YOUNG JAMES HERRIOT

THE MAKING OF THE
WORLD'S MOST FAMOUS VET

BY JOHN LEWIS-STEMPEL

BBC
BOOKS

This book is published to accompany the television series entitled *Young James Herriot*, first broadcast on BBC1 in 2011.

Executive Producer: Cameron Roach
Producers: Willy Wands, Kate Croft
Executive Producer BBC: Gaynor Holmes

1 3 5 7 9 10 8 6 4 2

First Published in 2011 by BBC Books, an imprint of Ebury Publishing.
A Random House Group Company

This paperback edition first published in 2012.

The Random House Group Limited Reg. No. 954009

Addresses for companies within the Random House Group can be found at
www.randomhouse.co.uk

A CIP catalogue record for this book is available from the British Library.

ISBN 978 1 849 90272 4

MIX
Paper from
responsible sources
FSC® C016897

The Random House Group Limited supports The Forest Stewardship Council (FSC®),
the leading international forest certification organisation. Our books carrying the FSC label are
printed on FSC® certified paper. FSC is the only forest certification scheme endorsed by the
leading environmental organisations, including Greenpeace. Our paper procurement
policy can be found at www.randomhouse.co.uk/environment

Commissioning editor: Albert DePetrillo
Project editor: Laura Higginson
Copy-editor: Clare Wallis
Illustrations: Mai Osawa
Production: Phil Spencer

Designed and typeset by seagulls.net
Printed and bound by CPI Group (UK) Ltd, Croydon, CR0 4YY

To buy books by your favourite authors and register for offers, visit www.randomhouse.co.uk

CONTENTS

INTRODUCTION

I write this surrounded by four dogs. Outside the window are ponies, cows, sheep, chickens, goats, ducks and a goose that escaped Christmas.

James Herriot would love it. But then James Herriot is to blame for it. As a child growing up in the Seventies, I was addicted to his books detailing his life as a country vet in Yorkshire. Not to mention the TV series and the films.

I even wanted to be a vet; alas my quite remarkable inability to do maths prevented that so I settled my imbibed love of animals by taking up my family's usual method of employment. Farming. Well, that and writing books. And yes, I was influenced in that course too by one James Herriot.

Reading James Herriot's books as an adult I was struck by their greatness. I do mean greatness. The 'heart-warming charm' of his books sometimes beguiles as to their perfection in characterization, construction and prose. Look at *If Only They Could Talk* or *It Shouldn't Happen to a Vet* with a critical eye. Herriot, it can be said without exaggeration, can be mentioned in the same hallowed breath as Thackeray, Maugham or his own favourite author, P.G. Wodehouse.

It will come as a surprise to many, as it did to me, to find that James Herriot, the man who gave his name to 'Herriot Country' in North Yorkshire, was actually born in another area of the North East, Sunderland. He was then taken at a few weeks old to live in Glasgow, where he was 'bred'.

And, his real name was James Alfred Wight; James Herriot was a pen name, conjured up to avoid the problem that vets were not allowed to write books in the 1970s in their own names because this could be construed as advertising.

It is the life of Alf Wight – he was always known by his middle name – from birth until his joining the famous veterinary practice of Siegfried Farnon in Darrowby at the age of 23 that is the subject of *Young Herriot*. Specifically, how a boy from a working-class shipbuilding family in Depression-era Glasgow became both a vet and a writer. Although James Herriot did not publish a book until 1966, when he was 50 and living in Thirsk (the real Darrowby), James Herriot, as veterinarian and as author, was made in Glasgow. His accomplishments were his own, but he would have been the first to acknowledge the part his family and his adopted city played in his success; 'With love to my mother,' reads the telling inscription in *Vet in Harness*, 'in dear old Glasgow town.'

Glasgow was also where Alf undertook his studies to become a vet. Glasgow Veterinary College in the Thirties was an eccentric institution. But Glasgow Veterinary College, like Glasgow itself, did something right: the two most successful veterinary authors in

British history both came from Glasgow, and both attended Glasgow Veterinary College. One was Alf Wight; the other was his friend Eddie Straiton, the 'TV Vet'.

James Herriot was fortunate, frankly, to train and practise as a vet when he did but all great writers are attended by a lucky star that puts them in the right place at the right time. He was witness to, and chronicler of, the very last days of an old order, in which vets did not yet have antibiotics and their farmer clients were not yet agri-businessmen. A pre-deluge society where the vet trailed an aura of black magic as he (and it was almost overwhelmingly he) arrived on small farms that seemed to grow, along with assorted livestock, colourful characters as a matter of course.

Antibiotics, in the shape of the sulphonamides, were discovered in a series of quiet experiments by Germany's IG Farben company in 1932. It is impossible to overestimate the impact of IG Farben's patented antimicrobial drugs. Vets went from making up colourful potions (frequently of dubious efficaciousness) to injecting colourless antibiotics of near miraculous nature. Within just ten years of Alf Wight leaving Glasgow Veterinary College in 1939, antibiotics had taken over, as Ken Mitchell who went to Edinburgh in 1944 to study veterinary science, discovered:

When I was a student I lived in a hostel with a lot of medical students. I was given penicillin, which was a trial drug, by them because I had laryngitis. By the time I had finished my course in 1949–50, antibiotics had become available not only in the human field but in the animal field as well and were starting to become well established in farm practise. You could now do surgery on the farm safely, for instance, and surgical operations such as caesarean sections became very common because you could use antibiotics to follow up and prevent infection.

With antibiotics, the vet's job changed utterly. Today it might be said that the vet's job is more about stopping illness starting than treating illness. In the words of Peter Jinman, President of the Royal College of Veterinary Surgeons:

Preventative medicine is the thing today. Rather than getting the vet out as a 'fire brigade', as in Herriot's day, the modern farmer has the vet out to discuss what the health plan will be for the species he's farming. That's not to say that vets have stopped doing fire-brigade work, but there's a definite emphasis change. Of course, the farmer's so much more knowledgeable now, he's a very trained individual. The farmer and the vet – it is one profession dealing with another profession today.

The antibiotic revolution was doubtless good for animals and for food production. It was less good for veterinary autobiography. Alf

Wight would claim that veterinary science in the Thirties and early Forties was harder work and less effective. 'But it was more fun.'

Who can argue?

It is this lost era of pre-War veterinary practice that the TV series *Young Herriot* brings to life. The show was the brainchild of Johnny Byrne; Johnny – who died in 2008 – wrote a number of episodes for *All Creatures Great and Small*. He knew Alf well, and felt that a 'James Herriot: The Early Years' about Alf's time at Glasgow Veterinary College in the Thirties would make a drama to equal and complement the original.

The TV series draws on Alf's unpublished novels, diaries, casebooks and historical records from the time to authentically recreate Glasgow and the activity inside Glasgow Veterinary College. But Johnny wanted a drama, rather than a documentary, something that would touch the screen magic of the Christopher Timothy-Robert Hardy-Peter Davison *All Creatures Great and Small*. Quite properly, this required some artistic license, so while the series is based on Alf's college years it is not a dotted i and crossed t accurate account of them. For *Young Herriot*, Johnny created a new friendship triangle reminiscent of Siegfried, Tristan and James – in *Young Herriot*, we have Whirly Tyson and Rob McAloon, both inspired by an archive of characters from the time. While Alf lived at home throughout his college years, Whirly, Rob and James live together in fictional Crannoch House run by the alluring young widow Mrs Monro. The stories in the series are taken from Alf's student casebook, but with a dramatization that enables them to come leaping to life in Glasgow and the countryside beyond.

TV drama is about the essence of things. A book to accompany the *Young James Herriot* series was called for, because a book has the luxury of explanation and elucidation for those in want of more information. The subtitle of this book is precise and deliberate: *The Making of the World's Most Famous Vet*. It is the biography of the real James Herriot, Alf Wight, but it is also the biography of the world in which he grew up and studied, of Glasgow and of veterinary medicine, because this world helps to explain him and his uniqueness.

It was another world, a world now long gone by.

JOHN LEWIS-STEMPEL

PROLOGUE
THROUGH THE ARCH

On the bright morning of 25 September 1933, 16-year-old Alf Wight clambered up the narrow canyon of Garnet Street in Glasgow's West End. So steep was the incline that the cobbles were oddly tilted, to allow the horses that hauled the coal up to the faded terraces and tenements to get a purchase with their metal shoes. A black Austin car coming down the hill rattled and skewed, its brakes smoking. Some of Alf's fellow panting pedestrians halted to catch their breath. He pressed on. An ardent follower of Lieutenant J. P. Muller's famous fitness regime and an athletics medallist at school, Alf Wight was not to be beaten by a hill. Besides, only a year ago he had been ill enough with diphtheria to come close to death: there was still pleasure to be had in every physical triumph over that disease, the name of which no-one spoke lightly in a crowded city such as Glasgow.

He was at the top and on the downhill. Almost there. Like every student starting college, his head ebbed with nerves and anticipation. There were other students scurrying along beside him, some probably to his college, but Glasgow School of Art (to which the young men wearing modish berets were presumably bound) and the dental school were both nearby on Renfrew Street.

Entering Buccleuch Street, Alf bore right and walked along until he reached his destination, number 83, a long, low building on the corner with Garnethill Street. It was not, he knew from attending his interview there, the most glorious seat of learning. It had no soaring spires, no shady quads, no honey-stoned façades. The building was dilapidated, covered with a job lot of yellow paint, and looked much like the Corporation utilities building it used to be. Now, though, 83 Buccleuch Street was, as the sign on the wall announced, 'Glasgow Veterinary College (Incorporated)', one of only four places in Great Britain in 1933 where a vet could be trained.

Bordered by Sauchiehall Street to the south and West Graham Street to the north, Garnethill was the Soho of Glasgow, its narrow-gorge streets known to all theatre artistes as the place for digs and to all creatives as the place to live. Over on Renfrew Street sat the Scottish beacon of Bohemianism, Charles Rennie Mackintosh's Glasgow School of Art building, with its eclectic architectural mix of *art nouveau*, austere Scottish baronial and iron industrial. For decades, Garnethill had been a refuge for foreigners arriving in Glasgow, and at 129 Hill Street was the unobtrusive Garnethill synagogue, constructed in 1879, the first purpose-built synagogue in Scotland.

'Raffish' was the word Alf attached to Garnethill, but the drumlin – precipitous enough for handrails to be installed so that those going up could pull themselves, those going down could steady

themselves – had not altogether lost bourgeois respectability. Glasgow Veterinary College at 83 Buccleuch Street sided Garnethill High School for Girls, a very proper educational establishment, which a Glaswegian Miss Jean Brodie would have recognized with a rebellious shudder and tried to liberate her 'gals' from.

Alf stepped towards the arched doorway of Glasgow Veterinary College, the former entrance for horses and carts. A small crowd of uncertain figures had gathered underneath: the new students. The seniors swanned in.

James Alfred Wight – as Alf was properly known – had already made several steps, as yet unrecognized, towards becoming James Herriot, the world's most famous vet and the teller of autobiographical tales about a country veterinary practice that would enthral millions. He had become fascinated with dogs, which was the prime reason he was about to go through the arch into Glasgow Veterinary College: he wanted to be a dog doctor. With self-sacrificing support from his parents – and by virtue of his acute intelligence – he had gone to one of Glasgow's best schools, where he had received the education that enabled him to enter veterinary college. He already wrote in a modest way, too: a diary, a couple of pieces for the school mag. Living on the absolute edge of Glasgow, he had become half a country boy, spending much of his spare time tramping the encircling green hills with his dog, Don. The city of Glasgow, that one-off metropolitan miracle of low mean streets and high exhilarating culture, had given him some things too, from a sharp self-deprecating humour to the Clyde-built inner steel that allows every Glaswegian to stick his or her chin out at adversity. There remained only the small matter of the training to actually be a vet.

In passing through the arch at 83 Buccleuch Street, Alf Wight would have his life transfigured. As Alf was about to discover, Glasgow Veterinary College's staff and students were to be counted amongst the most eccentric in academia. Despite – or more likely because of – its singularity, the institution made vets who were to be the most sought after in general practice. There was nowhere quite like Glasgow Veterinary College in the Thirties. But then, as Alf was also about to discover, there was nothing quite like veterinary medicine in the Thirties.

PART ONE

ABOUT A BOY

It was a world of noise.

3 October 1916: the Great War had begun two long years before, and as James Wight entered the world with a birth squall, men were leaving it screaming in the autumnal remains of the battle of the Somme. Among the early British casualties of the battle, when it was still a sunlit summer affair, was the baby's uncle, Alfred Wight, a sergeant in the 19th battalion of the Durham Light Infantry. The notice of Alfred Wight's death to his family was a black-edged telegram from the War Office. The telegraph boy knocked on many doors in the backstreets of Sunderland in 1916.

Alfred Wight was dead but his name lived on. It was inscribed on the skyline memorial to the fallen at Thiepval, and 'Alfred' was given as the middle name of the nephew he would never see. In fact, the baby boy born at number 111 Brandling Street – a red-brick terrace house named 'Fashoda' in the Roker area of Sunderland – would always be known as 'Alf', in preference to his proper first name, James, which came from his father, a 26-year-old ship plater. Like the nobility, working-class families in the early twentieth century passed down male names as if they were precious jewels.

* * *

Although Sunderland is slap on the north-east coast of England, far from the Western Front battlefields, the town rattled and reverberated with war sounds. There was sporadic shelling of the coast from German battleships and there were Zeppelin raids at night. Only six months before Alf was born, Zeppelin L-11 bombed the Star Cinema in Calvert Street, killing 22 people. The Zeppelins navigated to Sunderland by the fire-glow from the blast furnaces and foundries; everywhere in the town was the cacophony of factories turning out military materiel, of the ships being made in the yards on the banks of the Wear, where the clocking-on and clocking-off of the hobnail-booted workforce was signalled by the sounding of giant horns. In the 1840s, Sunderland had been the greatest shipbuilding centre in the world; by 1916 the town had declined in shipbuilding glory, but there were still 16 yards on the Wear, the tidal river that runs through Sunderland to the North Sea. The firms of J. L. Thompson and J. Blumer & Co. were almost on the doorstep of Fashoda.

* * *

Amid the noise of the shipyards and industrial Sunderland, other sounds lingered and beguiled. There was the Saturday afternoon roar of the crowd at Roker Park, home of Sunderland Association Football Club since 1898, when the 6th Marquess of Londonderry had turned the symbolic key to the entrance gates. Fashoda was almost within leather ball-throwing distance of the ground. Like his father, Alf would become a fanatical follower of 'The Black Cats'. 'I swear I never learned nursery rhymes,' Alf remarked, years later. 'I merely recited the names of the great players he [his father] had watched at Roker Park. As a very young child I knew of Buchan, Mordue, Holley, Cuggy and all the others my father idolised. To my father, anyone who played for Sunderland was a god in red and white.'

Football in 1916 was something more than a Saturday afternoon spectacle. Fifty years before, the public schools of England had taken the medieval brawl that was 'football' into the cloisters, and made it a game with rules, notably that of 'fair play'. Since then, public schoolboys of the 'muscular Christian' sort had returned the game to the people for their self-improvement. (Not a few clubs, among them Aston Villa, sprang from Sunday school; Sunderland AFC began as a club of the improvers of the people, school teachers.) In the year of the Somme, Association football was still the exhibition of model behaviour, a moral force for good.

There was also the sound of music. Alf's mother, Hannah – a force of nature, strong-willed, with fine, attractive features – also had a fine, attractive contralto voice, said by family members to cause them to cry because of its beauty. In those far-off decades at the beginning of the twentieth century, it was not unusual for families to gather around a piano (pianos then could be hired, as well as bought) in the flickering gaslit parlour, but even by the standards of the age, the Bells were musical. Hannah sang outside the home at concerts, and her parents belonged to all the Sunderland musical societies.

Music was the food of love between Hannah and Alf's father, James, who was more than the 'ship plater' he entered as his occupation on official documents. Despite losing an index finger in a youthful accident, James Wight was an accomplished pianist who played the organ in services at the Primitive Methodist Chapel on Williamson Terrace. Along with other manufacturing centres in the North, Sunderland had long been a centre of the evangelical, revivalist brand of John Wesley's creed, and James Wight must have been accustomed to formidable females like Hannah Bell; the Primitive Methodists had allowed women as preachers for 50 years.

As well as sitting at the organ in the plain brick chapel on Williamson Terrace, Jim Wight played piano and organ in the local cinemas. To perk up the new fangled silent 'flickers', film distributors sent 'cue sheets' out to cinemas containing lists of scenes and suggested pieces or styles of music to be played alongside them; *The Birth of a Nation*, D. W. Griffith's 1916 big-budget melodrama set in the American Civil War, even had a specially composed full score (by Joseph Carl Breil). But cue sheet or score, there was always ample opportunity for the cinema pianist to improvise, because the projectors broke down with audience-dismaying frequency. If the film caught fire or the projector bulb blew, the pianist filled in the unofficial interlude with a happy tune to distract the booing crowd in the stalls.

Someone like James Wight, dressed in a black dinner suit, playing a grand piano was the minimum musical staff in a cinema in 1916; bigger theatres had orchestras. Since films were on their way to becoming the entertainment medium of the people, cinemas were on their way to being the main employers of musicians. The pay for 'tinkling the old Joanna' in a cinema was £3 for a full week, but many musicians, like James Wight, were moonlighting from other jobs.

Until cinemas could be built or converted from existing buildings, films were shown in theatres. In Sunderland, the first sole-purpose cinemas were Monkwearmouth Picture Hall (a refitted chapel), the West End Electric Cinema, the Theatre de Luxe Cinema and the 2000-seat Havelock Cinema on the High Street. At the Sunderland Empire, the town's grandest venue, with its baroque 90-foot tower topped by a revolving steel globe bearing the figure of Terpsicore, seats in the stalls were 2d, and for 7/6d you could be the little emperor of all you surveyed from a box.

Aside from *Birth of a Nation*, the big film doing the rounds in 1916 was the British documentary about the death of a generation, *The Battle of the Somme*, the official record of the great advance, which sold twenty million tickets within six weeks of its release on 21 August. When it was shown to soldiers on rest, their chief complaint was that it lacked the furious noise of combat. Not even low-end 'Agitato Heavy' from Jim Wight's keyboard could simulate that.

Making music was the utter counterpoint to the work Jim Wight did in the shipyards, since few jobs in shipbuilding were more physically gruelling than plating. 'Ironfighters' was the suitable colloquialism for steel-trades workers like platers. A plater cut the steel plates that made up the ship's hull to rough size, trimmed them, and then curved them to perfection with hard, exquisite blows from a sledgehammer. Every job in shipbuilding had its noise, from the fusillade of the riveters to the splash of the welders; the noise of plating was barbaric gonging. No-one had ear protection; men went gradually deaf by the day.

After pounding the hull plates into shape, the plater's gang drilled lines of rivet holes with pointed steel rods, before 'shouldering' the plates from the 'shop' (a shed) to the hull on the open slipway, where the plates were hung ready for the riveters. Whether it was summer or winter, the job produced a blinding sweat under the ubiquitous flat tweed cap.

The work required strength, but also skill. Platers were artisans, men who took pride in their product. They could always be distinguished from the mass going through the yard gates by their metal tool-box. Inside were the tools of their trade: a hammer, centre punch, set square, protractor and level. Platers were trained to read the drawings coming out of the office. One fine day, James Wight himself would move from open yard to shipbuilder's office.

* * *

The plain brick chapel on Williamson Terrace where James played the organ was built in 1881; as John Betjeman wrote, such Nonconformist architecture showed 'more surely than any Victorian Established church ... what was the true architecture of the people. Not since medieval days had the people clubbed together to adorn a place of worship and this time it was not a shrine but a preaching house.'

Methodists 'clubbing together' to build a chapel was just one form of the self-organization beloved of the Victorian working-class into which Jim Wight and Hannah Bell were born. It is significant that Hannah's father, Robert Bell, and his wife Jane, owned rather than rented Fashoda; in the phrase beloved of Edwardian social commentators, the Bells were 'respectable working class'; the emphasis was, in the mind of the commentators, on 'respectable', but it should be on 'working', because there was no respectability without work. The Bells worked – and had worked upwards socially – with an ethic a Protestant would understand. Theirs was a world of friendly societies, Sunday schools, Mechanics' Institutes, reading rooms, trades unions. At Boldon, a mile or so away from Roker, the miners had a library funded from their own thin pockets, where the shelves boasted Walter Scott, Shakespeare, Milton, the Bible, the Brontës, Victor Hugo, Alexandre Dumas and George Eliot.

Sober, unpretentious, hard-working, auto-didactic, self-improving, cultured – small wonder that the British working class of the Victorian and Edwardian periods was the envy of the world. Alf Wight's parents would migrate from Methodism and even from their 'birth class', but they would not leave the moral and spiritual values learned there.

Hannah Bell and James Henry Wight were married on 17 July 1915 in that same Methodist chapel. There is a photograph of the wedding party, all suits, button-holes and bouquets: the Wights, as well as the Bells, were eminently respectable Wearside working class. But Hannah and Jim had dreams beyond Sunderland and the social rung on the ladder that birth had allotted them. They wanted careers in music.

It was Hannah who was the driver in the marriage, the glint of determination and focus there in the eyes in every monochrome snap. Jim was always the picture of gentle, open-faced amiability. Some of Hannah's relatives nicknamed her 'Duchess' for her airs and aspirations. It wasn't meant cruelly; the Bells, like the Wights, were a tight-knit supportive clan. It was just that Hannah wanted to go further up in the world, to improve herself.

If you are from the north of England in the second decade of the twentieth century, where do you go for the bright lights of a career in music? Across Britain stretches an invisible cultural barrier, and its line of latitude is just below Sunderland. A Hadrian's Wall of the mind. Above it is 'the North', below it 'the South'. When Scottish music-hall comics go on tour, they don't venture south of Wearside because nobody understands their humour or accents.

So, if you are from Sunderland in the 1910s and you want a career in music, you go to Glasgow, the Second City of the British Empire. Before they married, Hannah seems to have sent Jim off as a pathfinder to Glasgow, a city that had the advantage of offering both entertainment opportunities galore, plus the bread-and-butter of work in shipbuilding. In October 1914, Jim wrote to Hannah from Glasgow on a postcard:

I arrived here 10.10 today. Made tracks for Yarrows at once. Everything proved satisfactory.

Yarrows was a shipyard on the Clyde. Everything must indeed have proved satisfactory because Hannah and Jim moved to Glasgow immediately after their marriage. She only returned to Sunderland in October 1916 to have her baby in the cradle of her family.

Three weeks after Alf's birth, Hannah headed north again to where she and Jim had settled in Yoker, on Glasgow's north-west edge. From Roker to Yoker was a distance of 170 miles. It was there, in what he called 'dear old Glasgow town', that Alf Wight spent the first 24 years of his life.

SECOND CITY OF EMPIRE

'All through those thoughts there is one thing
that stands out like a beacon; the wonderful way
in which you put me first and gave me a
chance to be something in the world.'

Alf Wight, letter to his parents, November 1941, aged 25

When three-week-old Alf Wight arrived at the vaulting, glass-roofed Central Station in Glasgow in October 1916, he entered a metropolis like nowhere else in Britain. A clamouring city of 800,000 people, Glasgow was already showing, beneath the wartime spirit of unity, the split personality that would characterize it through the twentieth century. On the one hand it was the booming 'Second City of Empire', boasting the high culture of Charles Rennie Mackintosh, shipbuilding barons, and stylish Buchanan Street; on the other hand, street gangs like the Redskins were turning it into 'razor city', the Glasgow of blackened Gorbals tenements, Red Clydesiders and the variety-hall turns of Harry Lauder. The duality of Glasgow extended to its name because

Glaswegians could not agree on its meaning. Some insisted that Glasgow meant 'dear green place', from the Celtic *glas* (green) and *cu* (dear); James Cleland, writing in *The Annals of Glasgow*, was equally adamant that the name meant 'dark glen'. Even Glasgow's patron saint has two names – Mungo and Kentigern.

This split personality, though, marked an important truth about the place. The spectrum of human experience within its streets was broad, if not boundless. And Glasgow was dynamic. So dynamic, indeed, that in the early 1900s, many commentators queried whether Glasgow was truly a British city. With its confident high Victorian buildings, its grid of ruler-straight central streets, its brash manners and confidence, its brownstone tenement blocks, its 'subway' underground railway, its plethora of cinemas, its poor and huddled refugees from Ireland (more than 40 per cent of Glaswegians could claim roots in the Emerald Isle), Glasgow seemed American. When that inveterate explorer of Britain, H. V. Morton, reached Glasgow in 1912, he likened the city to Chicago; 20 years later, on his *Scottish Journey*, Edwin Muir was convinced that, 'In its combination of riches and tastlessness, upper-class Glasgow is very like the United States.'

The comparison with America is apt because modern Glasgow, like so many American cities, grew rapidly, a stone-and-mortar Topsy. Until the 1700s if people in Scotland, let alone in Britain, knew of Glasgow, they knew of it as a slumbering ecclesiastical town, whose first wooden church had been established in 525 by Mungo on the banks of the Molendinar Burn (a tributary of the Clyde that the Victorians turned into a sewer), and of its cathedral begun by Bishop John Achaius in 1114. In 1451, King James II had accorded the town a 'grant of regality' and solicited a Papal Bull to found the University of Glasgow, the fourth oldest university in Great Britain. Medieval Glasgow's population rose to around 4000, which crowded into timber and thatch houses around the cathedral, with some sprawl down to the shallow Clyde, with its thriving salmon fishing.

For three hundred years, Glasgow slept, until some enterprising merchants purchased 13 acres at Newark out in the Firth of Clyde and established Port Glasgow. Tobacco was the imported stuff on which Glasgow's rise to power was based; at Trongate in the city centre, the 'tobacco lords' had pavements exclusively for their own use. 'They were princes,' wrote chronicler John Strang, who

> *distinguished themselves by a particular garb, being attired, like their Venetian and Genovese predecessors, in scarlet cloaks, curled wigs, cocked hats, and bearing gold-headed canes.*

So was born the Glasgow habit of ostentation. So too the Glasgow habit of drinking. The nouveau riche tobacco merchants drank claret and whiskey in their clubs, coffee houses and homes (some employed servants specially to loosen the cravats of drunken guests, so they would not choke) while their lowly workers drank in taverns, or 'drinking shops', the back rooms of grocery stores.

The reign of the tobacco lords was brief; in 1786 David Dale brought mechanized weaving to the Clyde Valley, and cotton became king. Within a decade, Glasgow went from Daniel Defoe's 'cleanest and beautifullest, and best-built city in Britain, London excepted' to an industrial city where, one commentator observed in 1792, 'The traveller approaching this city, beholds before him, nothing but spires, buildings and smoke.'

Glasgow had entered the Industrial Revolution. Its population exploded: in 1801 Glasgow had 77,000 residents; by 1830 the population had nearly tripled to 201,000; and in 1901 Glasgow had 784,496 citizens within its burgeoning borders and was the most populous place in the kingdom, London excepted. It was also the 'Workshop of the World', because all the ingredients for heavy industry were to be miraculously found on the city's doorstep. In Lanarkshire there was iron ore and there was coal; there was also a ready supply of cheap labour in the shape of crofters cleared from the Highlands by 'improving' estate owners. These were joined by hungry Irish immigrants driven across the sea by the potato famines. The last ingredient necessary for Glasgow's rise to become 'Second City of Empire' was liquid. The water of the Clyde.

As the saying goes, 'Glasgow made the Clyde, the Clyde made Glasgow.' To deepen the Clyde so that bigger draught ships could reach right up into the city – the Port of Glasgow was always a halfway house sort of compromise – an English civil engineer, John Golborne, dreamed up a scheme in 1768 to dredge the sandbanks and narrow the river by means of jetties. Golbourne's plan was entirely successful; within a decade, coasting vessels were able to discharge Irish oatmeal at Broomielaw Quay in the heart of the city. A grateful town council gave Golbourne the Sassenach a present of £1,500 and a silver cup. However, the channel was still not deep enough to allow foreign-going vessels into Glasgow. Step forward the Scottish engineer Thomas Telford, who advised joining up the end of Golbourne's projecting groynes, and by 1818 transatlantic ships were regularly sailing up to the Broomielaw, turning Glasgow into a deep-water port. The river that runs through the city's heart is a canal, as artificial as Suez and Panama.

A deepened Clyde was more than a watery highway for trade; in 1812 the *Comet* was launched on the river, a little wooden steam paddleboat, which started up the holiday habit of taking a trip 'doon the watter'. So fantastically popular was the *Comet* that more steam ships were built in its wake. Shipbuilding was a new Glasgow craft, completely contingent on the newly deepened Clyde. In the sixteenth century, the town had boasted one boat builder. By the 1870s, the Clyde was building one-third of all British tonnage. And it had not nearly reached its ascendancy. The yards began to spread downstream, along the banks of the Clyde, from Govan (where Robert Napier had established the first yard to make hulls from steel instead of wood) to Partick, Whiteinch, Scotstoun … and Yoker.

* * *

Until 1877 Yoker was an inconsequential country village, whose singular point of interest was its distillery – cruelly hit by a Luft-waffe bomb in the Second World War, sending up a million pounds' worth of whiskey in flames – but in that year Govan shipbuilders, Messrs. Napier Shanks and Bell took over farmland with river frontage at the west end of the village. Other shipbuilding and repairing firms also found the greenfield sites of Yoker attractive, and John Shearer & Son, Barclay Curle & Co., J. & G. Thomson and John Brown & Co. all built yards on the river at Yoker. In 1906, the specialist warship builders Yarrow moved from the Thames to the eastern end of Yoker village, because as Alfred Yarrow observed, 'When you want apples, you go to Covent Garden, for meat to a meat market, and for ships you go to the North.' When James Wight wanted work in 1914, he was of the same mind as Alfred Yarrow, and went north, to Yoker on Glasgow's edge, to work in Yarrow's own yard.

A rented ground floor flat at number 2172 Dumbarton Road, Yoker, a four-storey red sandstone tenement block, was Alf's first home in Glasgow. Dumbarton Road is one of the major arteries of Glasgow, running west to Dumbarton itself and so long that it was the first road in Britain to need quadruple digits for addresses. Number 2172 is still there. Tenement buildings do not stand alone, but are joined to others, to cliff-wall pavements for six hundred yards with an overpowering solidity. All flats in a block have the same windows (an angular outward bay in the case of Dumbarton Road) and entrances; only the occasional small shop let into the ground floor disrupts the clone-like repetition of the tenements running down a road. The shops in the tenements next door to 2172 are now shuttered up, save for one convenience store with a bright yellow Paypoint sign.

Opposite 2172 is the site of the yard of the once mighty Barclay Curle, Scotland's main ship repairer, now gone. Three hundred yards downstream to the east, a grey Royal Navy warship peers from behind a line of new housing. Currently owned by BAE Systems, the Yarrow yard on Yoker's edge is one of the handful of Clydeside yards still living. Even so, there is only the faintest tinnitus of industry in Yoker on a workday in the twenty-first century.

In 1916, the riverfront of Yoker was alive with hammering, grinding, ships' horns sounding, cranes creaking, men shouting and trains running alongside Dumbarton Road to service the yards. So close were the gargantuan metal skeletons of the ships that they loomed over the wide cobbled road, blocking out the view from the tenements.

The sky over Yoker's Dumbarton Road was netted with wires to power tram 'caurs' running up and down the road, these emblazoned with the patriotic advice: 'To shave the boys at the Front, hand your old razors to the conductresses.' Or the patriotic plea: 'Bantams for the Front: 3,000 Wanted: Apply at Once 46 Bath Street.' Trams were also festooned with commercial advertisements for Fry's Pure Concentrated Cocoa, Colman's Mustard, Pear's Soap and Nestles' Milk. At night, the street flickered with gaslight, or at least it did until 12 o'clock. In response to possible Zeppelin raids, much of Glasgow's street lighting was extinguished from midnight and heavy curtains pulled over windows.

Night brought little relaxing silence to tenement dwellers. Although the broad streets were deserted, inside the tenement buildings were sick children crying, people arguing, someone using the landing closet and at weekends, parties.

Day or night, the air of Yoker was always tinged with the sulphurous smell of coal from the thousands of domestic 'ranges' (stoves) and fires in the tenements, from Yoker power station, from the Drysdale engineering works and from the shipyards themselves.

The tenement building in which the Wights lived was owned by a Mrs Isabell Jones of Golfhill Drive, Dennistoun. Like the other tenements in Yoker, it was purpose-built, either by the shipbuilding firms or by speculators. Since town councils did not then have the power to build houses, housing was a matter for private enterprise; because a thousand pounds spent on a tenement block could garner more in rents than a thousand pounds in a bank account could accrue in interest, the savvy and monied from all Renfrewshire and Lanarkshire invested in red stone Yoker tenements.

Glasgow was the most densely populated city in Europe. When Alf was a boy in the Second City, three-quarters of his fellow citizens lived in tenements, and three-quarters of all tenement flats were either single rooms ('single-ends') or two rooms ('room and kitchen'). Flats like the Wights', with two rooms and a kitchen/ sitting room, were for the slightly better off, costing about £12 a year in rent. Simply by walking past, you could tell that the Wights' tenement block was for the 'respectable working class', with its brown ceramic tiles in the entrance, and shoulder height green, black and yellow border. A 'wally close' it was called – 'close' being the communal doorway and 'wally' the Glaswegian vernacular for tiles. Among the Wights' neighbours were an engineer, Alex

Turnbull, and his wife, Gavin Brand, also an engineer, and William Carruthers, an engineering draughtsman, and his wife Eliza.

Not all were as lucky as the Wights. Across Glasgow to the east and south were the slums of the Gorbals, Plantation and Bridgeton, where the tenements were largely single rooms in 'made-down' (sub-divided) grand houses. It was not uncommon for whole families, plus lodgers, to live in a single-end, eleven to the room. Living conditions in a 'made-down' tenement were graphically described by William Bolitho, a South African journalist working for the *Guardian*:

We enter the Close. On each landing opens the water-closet, which the municipality installed thirty years ago. This is clean – the municipal are vigilant; but on average twenty-five persons share its use. In some houses this number is nearer fifty. On the other side of the tiny landing opens a long, impenetrably black gulf; the central corridor of five homes. We feel our way, knock at a door and enter, calling out 'Sanitary'. A small room, one side of which is taken up by the Scots' fireplaces, like an enclosed iron altar, with two hobs on which the teapot is kept everlastingly on the boil. The floor is worn wood, there are irregular square inches of frayed oilcloth. An enormous drabbled woman, who is dressed in dish clothes which do not show the dirt so plainly, however, as her face, explains the arrangement... She has five children, and the gas is kept burning all day at the glimmer. The elements are simple and human. There is the bed, set into a niche, deep, evil-smelling, strewed with heaps of the same material as her dress...

The shared lavatory was sometimes outside on the back court. An 1892 Act was supposed to force landlords to install indoor water closets but was not exactly successful: some tenement flats had outside loos as late as the 1960s.

The Gorbals, Glasgow's most famous slum, did not start out poor; initially the Gorbals – the name is thought to derive from the Gaelic 'gort an bhaile', meaning the town's field – was thoroughly middle class, but its elegance faded when the Irish, Highland and European migrants moved in. It was five minutes' walk from the wealth of the city centre – the Argyll *galleria* with its diamond merchants, Sauchiehall Street with its department stores – but in the Gorbals children went barefoot, and porage and broth were the principal meals. Bandy-legged rickets was the result. By the time of the First World War, the east and south side slums of Glasgow were already locked in a cycle of deprivation. As A. MacArthur and H. Kingsley Long observed in *No Mean City,* their classic novel of Glasgow life:

...the lads and lasses alike are driven to marriage in the slums by sheer disgust of their own homes and desire to start afresh in a 'hoose' of their own, roomy enough, though

it be no better than a 'single end'. Married, they have babies
in steady succession. If times are hard, they soon have to
take in a lodger or two. In any event, before a dozen years
have passed they have set up a home no whit different from
the ones their parents made and soon their children begin
to think of a similar escape from it.

Buildings in the Gorbals, as in much of Glasgow, were uniformly black over yellow or red stone; before the Clean Air Act, the only time you could see the hills from the city centre was in July during the annual Fair Holiday, when the factories closed. Sometimes the smog was so thick that the unwary walked into the Clyde and drowned.

Yoker was not the Gorbals. Yoker still had a green lung along its northern, non-riverside edge. And when the baby Alf Wight moved into the two-room ground floor flat at 2172 Dumbarton Road, the Gorbals had already been abandoned by money, which was following the spread of the shipyards west along the Clyde. Partick, Whiteinch, Scotstoun and Yoker were all booming. When novelist John Buchan wanted to prove the wartime bustle of Glasgow in *Mr Standfast*, where did he send hero Richard Hannay? Where else but Dumbarton Road? There Hannay was 'amazed at the number of able bodied fellows about, considering that you couldn't stir a mile on any British front without bumping up against a Glasgow battalion.

Then I realised that there were such things as munitions and ships, and I wondered no more.'

During the Great War there was always a ship to build for the Royal Navy or for the merchant fleet being depleted by the Kaiser's U-boats only 40 miles away in the Western Approaches of the Atlantic; between 1914 and 1918 Yarrow's yard built no less than 47 warships for the Admiralty. It was the highwater of shipbuilding on the Clyde, and platers like Jim Wight, the aristocrats of the yards, were taking home as much as £4/18s for a 50-hour week. Yarrow fed the stomach, but the Wights had moved to Glasgow for the good of their souls, to further their careers in music. And Glasgow was entertainment city.

If Glasgow ever dominated a branch of entertainment, it was music hall. Neil Kenyon, Jack Buchanan and Nellie Wallace all belonged to Glasgow, and Edinburgh boy Sir Harry Lauder was adopted by Mungo's city (or he adopted it) and he was the most popular vaudeville comedian in the world. When Sir Harry Lauder appeared in Glasgow, people queued for hours to hear him sing '*I Love a Lassie*', '*Stop Yer Ticklin, Jock*', '*Roamin' in the Gloamin*', '*Donald Where's Yer Trewsers*' and, of course, '*I Belong to Glasgow*', with its famous chorus:

I belong to Glasgow, Dear old Glasgow town;
But what's the matter wi' Glasgow,

For it's goin' roun and roun!
I'm only a common old working chap,
As anyone here can see,
But when I get a couple of drinks on a Saturday,
Glasgow belongs to me.

Music hall's lofty peak was 1916. The Empire Theatre (showing 'Shell Out – The Wonderful Revue') was the largest hall outside London's Savoy, and the Alhambra, the Coliseum, the Palace in the Gorbals and the Olympia in Bridgeton were all packing them in. At rough establishments like Pickard's Panopticon Music Hall on Trongate – no longer the playground of merchants – where Stan Laurel made his debut, punters chucked rivets at the artistes they did nae like. Such was the penalty of a poor performance in a ship-building town.

There were also a hundred cinemas in Glasgow by 1917, the highest percentage per head of population of anywhere in Britain. Anywhere in the world outside America, come to that. The first building to open exclusively for the showing of films was Pringle's in Sauchiehall Street in 1907 with 200 seats, but quickly the trend for cinemas became for palace-sized establishments with a touch of luxury. So, the Picture House had a goldfish pool and cages of singing birds, and La Scala offered fish teas and afternoon teas. 'If it's Good it is Green's' was the slogan of George Green, the Lancashire circus-owner who morphed into the city's movie-house mogul, and whose Green's Playhouse was the biggest cinema in Europe, seating 4368 in velvety comfort.

George Green employed James Wight as a pianist at his 1100-seat Picturedrome cinema at 21 Govan Street (now Ballater Street) in the Gorbals. It was a four-mile tram journey there and back in the evening. There were picture houses much closer, such as the Paladium and Victoria in Scotstoun so presumably Green was offering top pounds, or the Gorbals job was a foot in the orchestra pit of the Green empire. Or perhaps Hannah, under her stage name of 'Anna Bell', had the opportunity of singing in the intervals. Whatever, Jim along with all the rest of the male world travelling on the clattering double-deck tram 'caurs' would have wondered at the new breed of person clipping the tickets. With so many of its male employees away at the war, Glasgow Tramways enrolled 700 female conductresses, dressing them out in green straw hats and long Black Watch tartan skirts.

It was becoming a strangely female world. Scotstoun, next door to Yoker, had started the phenomenon of woman 'posties'; the Grand Central, a restaurant 'de luxe', now featured the Belgian Ladies Band from the Liège Conservatoire; a Scottish training school for women police officers had opened in Charing Cross, the graduates of which were kept busy arresting illegal distillers; the 'shebeeners' included women too, such as Govan's Sarah Gillam, who copped a £30 fine from the city's court for half a bottle of home-made whiskey. Meanwhile, women war workers – 'the shell belles' – were earning a whacking £3/5s a week and, to the bemusement of the city's burghers, had taken to frequenting the best emporia on the grand streets of the city centre, which were thronged with people, trams and horse-drawn carriages in these days of money. There was perhaps always a tempting of fate in the way that Glasgow threw money around during the Great War. Certainly the boom went bust.

When Jim Wight had walked through the dock gates of Yarrow's yard in 1914 and was signed on by a foreman, he was one of 60,000 men working in the Clyde's shipyards and marine engineering shops. But the war had artificially inflated the order book – of Yarrow's in particular. Cancellation of Admiralty work was met with protests in the Yarrow's yard. To no avail. In 1919, one year after the war's end, the number of men employed in the Clyde yards was 43,000. One after the other, the yards on the Clyde ceased production, as did all the engineering shops and steel foundries dependent on them. Yarrow's itself closed temporarily, and was only reborn by some sporadic Admiralty orders and a diversification into the making of land boilers.

Jim Wight was among those laid off, leaving him to join the throngs of shipyard workers standing at six o'clock each morning outside the gates, hoping to catch the attention of one of the 'bastards in bowlers' – the foremen. One retired shipyard worker from Browns told Alan McKinlay, the editor of the Clydebank oral history project *Making Ships, Making Men*:

If you were a riveter or whatever, you used to go down in the morning and wait outside the foreman's office and he would say 'you, you and you' and give you a start. Sometimes the foreman would walk up and down the lines of men waiting for work without saying a word, not even a grunt – which most of them were capable of. That meant there was no work for you that day. They were just reminding you that they had all the power and you had none.

If there was no work, men signed on at the 'Buroo' (Bureau) for their 'dole' three times a week. Unemployment in Glasgow rocketed; in 1921 unemployment grew in the city by 1000 a day, and the sight of people digging in the abandoned coal bins on the city's edge and men lounging listlessly on street corners became seared in the city's memory. For something to do, the so-called 'gentry of the corner' would go singing in the back courts of the tenements. One of their ditties began:

Winter is coming, the night is beastly derk
The erc lights are fizzing in the West End Perk
All of the erc lights fizz like gingerade
End aih'm beneath your window
With this chairming serenade.

If they were lucky, someone would throw down a ha'pence. To make them go away.

It was against this background of economic ruination that the legend of 'Red Clydeside' was born. Although the Great War had seen strikes in the shipyards, including Yarrow's, the real trouble came in 1919 with a demand for a 40-hour week, which the employers refused. At a massive demonstration in Glasgow's George Square on 31 January 1919 in support of the shipyard workers, the Red Flag was unfurled. Police and trade unionists fought a pitched battle in which 53 people were injured. The Liberal Coalition Government sent in armed soldiers and tanks, and for a brief, panicky moment, class warriors on both sides thought that the Bolshevik Revolution of October 1917 was near to being repeated on 'Black Friday' in Glasgow. The strike was almost immediately called off, but the fear of its consequences remained. *The Times* of London reported:

> *Thousands of soldiers wearing steel helmets and full service kit were brought into Glasgow yesterday morning, and the hooligan element responsible for the bottle-throwing, window-smashing and looting on Friday has disappeared from the streets. I do not think there will be any recurrence of disorder. Those who now speak for the strikers [Emmanuel] Shinwell has been arrested at his home in Govan, and with [David] Kirkwood and [William] Gallagher is detained under remand at Duke Street prison – instead of talking of unconstitutional methods are asking*

*the authorities to prove one instance of illegal conduct by
the men. In their paper the* Strike Bulletin, *today they say –
'It seems as if the Government want an opportunity to use
arms against the workers on the Clyde, but we can assure
them the workers have no desire or intention of providing
such an opportunity. The workers are well aware of what
the Government want and are not so foolish as to fall into
the trap set so carefully to ensnare them.'*

*This is ingenious, but it may serve the purpose of
restraining young hotheads from rash action. The looters,
who serve one purpose of the revolutionary movement
behind the strike itself, may be trusted to keep in hiding
while the troops guard the city.*

Clydeside's reputation for being 'Red' extended to parliamentary
politics. In the general election of 1922, ten of Glasgow's seats were
won by the Independent Labour Party, under the leadership of
James Maxton and John Wheatley. An enormous demonstration in
St Enoch Square saw the successful ILP members off on the night
train for London. But their noble manifesto, dedicated to the 'unity
of the nations of the world ... happiness of the people of these
islands', was soon to come under pressure of the *realpolitik* prac-
tised at Westminster. Unable to deliver on its rosy promises, the ILP
lost members right (Labour Party) and left (the Communist Party).

Yet Glasgow was never as politically red as it was painted. During the early years of Alf's life in the Second City, Glasgow's problem wasn't wee red men; it was the wee hard men – and women – taking to drink to drown their sorrows about the Depression. A popular children's skipping song of the time asked the question:

Does yer maw drink wine?
Does she drink it a' the time?
Does she ever get the feelin'?
That she's gonni hit the ceilin'?
Does yer maw drink wine?
Does yer maw drink gin?
Does she drink it oot a tin?
Does she ever get the feelin'
That she's gonni hit the ceilin'?
Does yer maw drink gin?

One particular drink was the curse of the Glasgow unemployed classes: a cheap red wine laced with methylated spirits known as 'Red Biddy', 'Johnny Jump Up' or 'Jake'. So toxic was the cocktail that the injurious effects of the drink were brought to the attention of the House of Commons more than once. Red Biddy cost 7d a bottle. In the depression-blighted East End, unemployed men were reported to be addicted to another drink in the Twenties, meths boiled with brown vinegar, which was consumed by Glaswegians at 1s a gill.

'Most of my boyhood companions finished up as wine drinkers,' recalled Eddie Straiton, who would join Alf as a teenage student at Glasgow Veterinary College and be a fixture in Alf's life for over fifty years. 'If they didn't have at least average intelligence, they simply had no chance. There was absolutely no future. With parents on the dole, their only prospects when they left school were endless days of lounging around street corners and billiard rooms until they were old enough to sign on at the "buroo" – the unemployment exchange. Inevitably many, like their parents, turned to drink.'

As a student, Alf would have to hide the smell of drink on his breath from his Temperance-inclined mother. But many a Glaswegian boy would have preferred a Maw who was a Methodist to a Maw who was drinking Red Biddy.

* * *

Glasgow spawned gangs: the Duke Street Boys, Baltic Fleet, the Nunnies, the San Tong, the Beehives, the Calton Entry, the Bingo Boys, the Govan Team, the South Side Stickers, the Cheeky 40, the Kent Stars, the Coburg Erin, the Romeo Boys, the Dirty Dozen, the Lollipops, the Savoy Arcadians, the Billy Boys, the Norman Conks ... all had their nasty, brutish and short reigns of infamy on the streets of the East End and the South Side.

Some gangs owed their allegiance to a particular stretch of cobbles – the Nunnies were from Nuneaton Street – others to a faith. This was Glasgow, after all, sectarian city of Orange, sectarian city of Green. Of the city's two most infamous gangs of the inter-war era, the Billy Boys and the Norman Conks, one was Proddy and one was Papist. The battle cry of the Billy Boys was:

> *Hullo, Hullo*
> *We are the Billy Boys*
> *Hullo, Hullo*
> *You'll know us by our noise*
> *We're up to our knees in Fenian blood*
> *Surrender or you'll die*
> *For we are*
> *The Brigton Derry Boys*

Brigton was the local spelling of Bridgeton. A version of the song became the anthem of Glasgow Rangers Football Club until in 2006 UEFA instructed the club to make public announcements prohibiting its singing. Elsewhere in Britain, football was a cohering celebration of working-class life; in disintegrating, deprived Glasgow it was something to be fought over between the Protestant fans of Rangers and the Catholic fans of Celtic, the matches between them ending in bloody, kicking trouble with monotonous frequency.

The Billy Boys' leader in the Thirties was Billy Fullerton, one of Glasgow's 'razor kings', so named for their proclivity in using a cut-throat razor on their enemies. A fellow 'razor king', John Ross, was taken before the judge in 1931, where *The Scotsman* reported:

Amazing sidelights regarding the gang problem in Glasgow were given when a 22-year-old youth, known to his associates as the 'razor king' appeared before Lord Anderson in the North Court for sentence on a charge of assault. Accused was John Ross, stated to be a section leader of the 'Billy Boys' gang, and he pleaded guilty to a charge of having on November 27, while acting in concert with a number of unknown men in James Street, Bridgeton, assaulted William Rankin of 125 Main Street, struck him on the face, knocked him down and kicked him, in consequence of which he was severely injured.

Moving for sentence, Mr Taylor said that [the] accused was known as the 'razor king' and he was a leader of one of the gangs of brutal and cowardly hooligans who infested certain districts of the city. The gang was known as the 'Billy Boys' and a short time ago it was 800-strong. It had now been reduced to about 400 ... Outlining the circumstances of the case, Mr Taylor explained that the assaulted man was in a picture house when some small quarrel arose between him and a girl, whose seat he was supposed to have occupied. The girl was apparently connected with the gang, and when the picture house was closed and the people were coming out, she passed the word to those members of the gang who were available. When Rankin went out he was pushed down the steps, struck from behind and knocked down by members of the gang.

While Rankin was lying on the ground he was kicked and assaulted. Indeed, at one time it looked as if he might be kicked to death, and a girl who was in the crowd, thinking he would be killed, very pluckily threw herself upon him as he lay on the ground and endeavoured to protect him as best she could until the arrival of the police. Rankin's injuries were fairly serious and he was taken to the Royal Infirmary for treatment ... Continuing, Mr Taylor said the two previous convictions admitted by the accused arose out of his activities as a gangster. The first one was one of assault by stabbing, and the second, which was a common assault, was committed on one of the female members of the gang, who had mislaid one of the razors from which he derived his name of the 'razor king'.

His Lordship sentenced Ross to 18 months' imprisonment.

Fullerton and Ross were the real-life models on which Johnnie Stark, the protagonist of No Mean City, was based. No Mean City began as a rambling story from the typewriter of an alcoholic Gorbals baker, Alexander McArthur, who lived on Waddell Street, close to the Southern Necropolis. In 1934, McArthur sent off the manuscript to Longman's, the publishers. Longman's saw nothing impressive in the writing or the plot but was so mesmerized by McArthur's revelations about the Gorbals' razor gangs, prostitutes, tenements and bedbugs that the company asked H. Kingsley Long, one of its professional readers, to look at the manuscript. A journalist on *The People*, Kingsley Long immediately packed his bag and went up to Glasgow to collaborate with McArthur on what would become *No Mean City: A Story of the Glasgow Slums*, the red-raw story of 'bullet-headed' Johnnie Stark, son of a violent father and downtrodden mother, who becomes the local 'Razor King'. Long chose the novel's title from the King James Bible, Acts 21:39, 'I am … a Jew of Tarsus, a city in Cilicia, a citizen of no mean city.'

No Mean City outraged decent Glasgow with its docu-drama depictions of sex and violence. Libraries were forbidden to stock it. The *Glasgow Evening Times* refused to review it. Even so, people read it – its total sales are estimated at about 750,000 – and those who did were shocked, not just by the character's amorality, but by the pervading sense of hopelessness. No matter what route the characters took to escape the slum, be it Johnnie's violence, his brother's espousal of the class struggle, his friend's dancing, no-one did. The slum reclaimed them all. In a terrible case of life imitating art, McArthur, unable to repeat the success of *No Mean City*, sank into alcoholism and eventually took his own life in 1947, downing a bottle of disinfectant, throwing himself off a bridge into the Clyde to crawl out on the towpath and lie like a beached fish. Only two people attended his funeral, both journalists.

The gangs were clustered in the East End and South Side, but there were gangs reported in Cowcaddens, Maryhill and Anderston, and Partick. Occasionally, though, the gangs erupted out of their slums to brawl in the city's *palais de danse* and cinemas. Some of the 'rammies' were arranged like a mass duel. After one running street war in June 1931, the *Glasgow Evening Times* reported:

> The spear of a swordfish and a wicked-looking Gurkha knife were among the number of weapons taken possession of by the police following an alleged gang fight in Kerr Street, Bridgeton, yesterday afternoon. The 'battlefield' was strewn with weapons after the fight … a piece of copper tubing … a brass-headed poker … a cudgel two feet long with a knob of wood as thick as the head of a drumstick … a wooden baton … an axe weighing 1½ lb … a steel file two feet long … a bayonet-like knife … and an iron rod three feet long, with a hook at each end.

It was widely and popularly believed that the gangs existed merely to fight their like and they never harassed 'ordinary' Glaswegians, they loved their Maws, and one could leave the door of the 'hoose' open in a street 'owned' by the gang because a larcenous thought never passed through their scarred heads. Actually, the gangs may not have been composed of Mister Big criminal masterminds, but all ran low-level felonious 'enterprises', chiefly protection rackets, whereby corner shopkeepers paid a 'pension' or got their windaes smashed. There was no honour among the gangs. If one of their number was fined or needed bailing, his fellows demanded money from householders, local businessmen and passersby.

Nobody in Twenties and Thirties Glasgow walked the streets without some fear of gang boys or 'neds'. When Alf was studying at Glasgow Veterinary College in 1934, a running gang fight in neighbouring Cowcaddens forced pedestrians to take shelter in shops and closes. Eventually, the city's authorities decided that the reign of the wee hard men must be ended and in 1931 recruited Percy Sillitoe as Chief Constable. The philosophy of Sillitoe, who had previously 'busted' the gangs of Sheffield, was simple: 'There is only one way to deal with the gangster mentality. You must not show you are afraid.' Sillitoe recruited to the city's police force – at 1500 strong the second biggest in Britain – Highlanders and rural men of imposing size (most famously Olympic wrestler Archie MacDonald), and kitted them out with batons and a distinctive diced black-and-white cap band, 'Sillitoe tartan' as it became known. Percy Sillitoe's Braveheart constables then proceeded to wade into the gangs at every opportunity, with the Chief Constable ensuring that judges passed hefty sentences on anybody apprehended. He also got rid of corrupt magistrates. The tipping point came in the late Thirties when Billy Fullerton was arrested in the middle of a melee and convicted of being drunk in charge of a child. Ten months in Barlinnie Prison ensued. With Fullerton gone, the Billy Boys lost their aura of invulnerability, and the era of gang rule was soon over. Sir Percy Sillitoe left Glasgow with the unofficial title of 'Hammer of the Gangs' and ended up as Director General of MI5.

It was as these storm clouds of economic depression gathered over Glasgow that the education of Alf began. On 30 August 1921, when Alf was two months shy of his fifth birthday, he passed his first day at Yoker Primary School. A hop-skip-and-jump along Dumbarton Road from 2172, and past the Auld Hoose pub, Yoker Primary, founded in 1876, was a low, stone Victorian building cornering Kelso Street. Boys entered through one gate, girls through another. Alf's seven years at the school were under the tutelage of William Malcolm MA, who was nicknamed 'Beery' by his charges on account of his florid visage, suggestive that its owner was partial to a pint of 'heavy'. But then nearly every schoolchild in Glasgow was convinced his or her headmaster drank. As the children's rhyme had it:

Oor wee school's the best wee school,
The best wee school in Glesca.
The only thing that's wrang wi' it
Is the baldy-heided maister.

He goes tae the pub on a Setterday night,
He goes tae church on Sunday,
An' prays tae God tae gie him strength
Tae belt the weans on Monday.

Alf's favourite subjects at Yoker Primary were English and History, the latter taught by the inspirational Mr Paterson, who liked to re-enact British history's best moments, from chopping off the 'heid' of Charles I to chopping off the 'heids' of the Sassenachs at Bannockburn, using his cane for a sword. History and English would long remain Alf's favourite subjects. (His *worst* subject at Yoker, as in life, was Maths.) The school day was from 8.45 am until 4pm, with an hour for lunch. In the yard at break times, Alf played football, 'British bulldogs', 'cuddie hunch', 'spin the pirie' and Bools (marbles). He also met the boy from Kelso Street called Alex Taylor who would become a friend for life. Indeed, so close was the friendship between Alf and Alex – widely known as Sandy, appropriately enough given his beach-blond hair – that 60 years hence Alex and his wife would retire to Yorkshire to live near Alf and his wife. Alex would even be godfather to Alf's son.

Like the primary school, Yoker Church belonged to the building boom that came to Yoker with the Victorian expansion of the ship-yards, when the village's population shot up from 535 in 1871 to about 20,000 in 1903. The foundation stone of Yoker Church was laid in 1897, and for most of Alf's childhood the Reverend William

Walls was the minister there, his 14-year incumbency beginning in 1921. By the account of *Both Sides of the Burn*, the local history of Yoker, Walls 'worked tirelessly among the people of the parish' during the Depression, and the church congregation was at full capacity. Among those sitting on the bare oak pews on Sundays were Alf and his parents; although Hannah and Jim were born and bred Methodists, in Yoker they attended the Presbyterian services of Yoker Church and Alf, according to his daughter Rosie Page, 'thought of himself as being brought up a Presbyterian'. Why did the Wights take the Presbyterian option? Aside from its convenience to 2172, Yoker Church was likely more to Hannah's social taste: there was a different class of person at prayer than at chapel. It was more middle class.

Whatever class a man was, he prayed for work whilst sitting on the pews of Yoker Church. During the early 1920s, 'Pop', as Alf called his father, was 'bouncing in and out of jobs'. Laid off from the yards – a blow for a proud man – he always found something, though. In 1926, the year of the General Strike, another fractious episode in Glasgow's history, he seems to have finally given up being a plater, entering his occupation on the city returns as a joiner.

He was fortunate, of course, to have that musical string to his bow, to be able to play music for money. Aside from leading the orchestra at the Govan Picturedrome, he played with the 'Glenafton Singers' and with the Glasgow Society of Musicians he performed all over the city. When the talkies, beginning with Al

Jolson's *The Jazz Singer* in 1927, looked set to kill live music in the cinemas, he played during the intervals, entertaining the punters as they queued for their ice-creams from the girl with the tray hanging from her neck.

Then there were the dances. After being music hall city, and cinema city, Glasgow became dance city. To put the Slump behind them, even if only for a brief hour, the people of Glasgow swung it out to the latest hot stuff coming in from America: the Tango, the Black Bottom and the Charleston. Whether it was in pub back rooms or in elaborate *palais de danse* ballrooms such as the Plaza at Eglinton Toll (multi-coloured lighting system, steel-sprung floors), dances needed someone on the piano, as well as the trombone and sax. By 1930, Glasgow (population 1 million) had 59 dances halls, while London (population 8 million) had 260.

The Wights' family finances, however, were not just a matter of Pop's efforts. In the dead economic years of the Twenties, Hannah sang for the family's suppers. She also began dressmaking, at which she excelled – and at which she made considerably more than pin money. Indeed, she soon had a veritable industry on her skilled hands, requiring several seamstresses and a maid, Sadie. Hannah's clients included the Glasgow great and good, such as Lady Ernest Field. Not many houses on Dumbarton Road would have enjoyed a maid, and a Christmas-card list that included the titled.

As a result, Alf was almost unscathed by the Depression, cocooned by his parents' love and hard work. When the Wights did not have work, they worked at getting work.

There is a photograph of Alf at Yoker Primary aged nine. He is smiling, and radiates self-assurance. He is conspicuously well turned out in a jacket, shirt and tie (as is Alex Taylor, resplendent in a sailor suit) and wears the look of someone who expects good things to happen in life. There are others in the photograph who, judging by their faces and apparel, do not.

In the same year, 1925, that Alf was snapped smiling in the yard at Yoker Primary, 'TV vet' Eddie Straiton started his first job, delivering milk with Jock the milkman at Clydebank for the princely

weekly wage of threepence. Straiton was aged eight. The job began
at four in the morning:

*My bare feet beat a tattoo on the pavement in an effort to
keep warm and the ice-cold gusts of wet wind searched
rudely under my short kilt. Goose pimples ribbed my rump
like rough sandpaper. The oil lamps of the milk float loomed
out of the dark and the old mare slowed down to big Jock's
suppressed 'Whoaa lass', while I swung myself on to the
tattered sacking that provided a seat beside the milkman's
massive form. He reeked of sour milk and cow dung.*

*'Rest yer arse there, laddie, and we'll dae Rannoch Street
first.' Rannoch Street was only slightly less poverty-stricken
than Sloan Avenue, which housed myself and many similar
urchins, all of whom constantly sought the very scarce part-
time jobs as a vital economic necessity. I was lucky; Jock's
regular helper had been sacked for 'drinkin' the mulk'.*

*In ten-gallon churns at the rear of the float slopped the
cargo of milk, and rattling in front was a pile of milk cans
with long handles. It was pitch dark but I knew they were
there. I had passed Jock's milk cart nearly every day since
toddling to school.*

*The work was hard, especially on an empty stomach.
My puny arms ached with the effort of carrying a full half-
gallon can up a 'close' – three flights of stairs. Most families*

lived in three-storey stone-built tenements, three houses on each floor. The tenants left money in jugs or cups outside their doors, one penny for a pint, a ha'penny for a half and a farthing for a teacupful.

After only three closes, Straiton found his heart breaking for the poverty of the people. When he reached the McCaffertys' in Glenville Street he could bear it no more: the father, broken by years of poverty, had drowned himself in the canal a month before, leaving Mrs McCafferty with eight children. 'I stared at the empty half-pint jug,' remembered Straiton. 'Inside there was no money, no note – nothing.' He secretly paid for Mrs McCafferty's milk himself, dropping his ha'penny Christmas present in Jock's money bag.

He then went to school.

*   *   *

Outside school, Alf enjoyed an early childhood almost scripted from the pages of *Boy's Own Paper*. Yoker might have been a ship-building village, but it was a shipbuilding village on Glasgow's absolute edge. (In fact, Yoker wasn't officially incorporated into Glasgow until 1926.) Beyond Kelso Street, five hundred yards from Alf's tenement, lay open country, and during Alf's first years in Yoker cows still wandered on to Dumbarton Road. He played 'Moshie' (flicking marbles into holes), kicked a football around on the fields and raced around on his Colson 'Fairycycle', after Pop helped him learn to ride. A 'Fairycycle' was a small-wheeled safety bicycle that was the object of green-eyed envy. Colson's advertisements declared:

Happy are the owners of Fairy Bikes – Velocipedes, Scooters, Tricycles, Coasters – each ride so gracefully, speedily and safely. Only Fairy Bikes are made exactly like you want them and last the way your parents hope they will.

Playtime is always joytime on a Fairy. What fun you can have! Out in the glorious sun, riding here and there in the fresh air, building strong, healthy bodies.

Owning a bike was a sure-fire way of getting sweets from other kids, because the city-wide standard bribe for a go on a bike was 'I'll give ye a sweetie for a shot on yer scooter.'

With a penny, rather than a sweetie, clutched in his hand he went to the Saturday matinees at the cinema, of which there were three close by: the Gaiety, the Empire and the Pavilion. On Saturday afternoons in winter, Alf stood with his father at Holm Park on Dock Street and shouted for the local football team, Yoker Athletic FC. Throughout the Twenties and Thirties, Yoker Athletic scored success after success in the junior division, winning the Scottish Intermediate Cup, the League Championship, the Glasgow

Charity Cup, the Elder Cup and in 1932–3, glory of glories, the Scottish Junior Cup. ('Whe Ho', as Yoker Athletic supporters say.)

Some of the notables in 'the Athletic' teams included Bobby Finan (later Blackpool and Scotland) and Sam English (Rangers and Northern Ireland). Jim would also take Alf to see Partick Thistle – just down the road – where one day Alf's Yoker schoolmate, Jackie Husband, played and eventually managed. There were also excursions to Rangers at Ibrox and Celtic at Hampden Park.

Inside the high-roomed flat at 2172, switching on the science-fiction phenomenon of electric lights, Alf played with Meccano and read books. Charles Alden Selzer's Wild West novel *"Drag" Harlan*, about a vigilante cowboy with 'the snakiest gun hand', was an early favourite to read by himself. And, of course, while Alf read, there would be the sound of music. Jim liked classical music, but also jazz and popular tunes ('Life on the Ocean Wave', 'Meet Me on the Back Porch'), which he would play on the grand piano he had shipped from Sunderland. There was also a wind-up gramophone in the kitchen-cum-sitting-room at 2172 Dumbarton Road, and on the turntable Jim would lay thick 78s of Caruso singing 'Vesti la Giubba' from *I Pagliacci* and listen again and again to the great tenor's voice ringing out through the ear-shaped speaker. When the player ran down, he would leap up to crank the handle. Not for Jim a raucous evening in the bar of the Auld Hoose pub getting 'legless'; instead he sat before the piano and gramophone, losing himself in music. Mrs Wight's musical tastes were no less deep, but they were more austere; she liked classical music and hymns. Together the Wights would attend musical concerts far and wide, the boy in tow ('Mother carting me in a shawl through railway barriers so that I could go for less fare').

From the age of six Alf had piano lessons – from his father, alas, which proved a rare source of friction between them. Alf failed to practise regularly and Pop set high standards, making the boy play Scarlatti's sonatas. Indeed, Pop hoped that Alf might make the grade as a professional musician.

At the age of 13, J. A. Wight made his debut as concert pianist, playing at the Clydebank Town Hall. The piece performed was 'Polish Dance No. 1' in E-flat minor by the Polish-German composer Xavier Schwarenka. It was the beginning ... and also the end. Alf never again performed on such a grand stage, his father apparently giving up the struggle with the lesson-resistant teenager. However, Alf carried on playing the piano for his own amusement, and music would interest him for the rest of his life. One consequence of growing up in a house of music was Alf's exotic choice of the pseudonyms Siegfried and Tristan for the Sinclair brothers in the Herriot books. In *If Only They Could Talk*, Alf surely writes with his own father in mind when he attributes the names to the pater's love of Wagner. Alf also betrays the home-steeping in Wagner by his ability to make the knock-on jokes about Wagnerian names:

'*Anyway, it could have been worse. Wotan, for instance.*'
'*Or Pogner.*'

One day during Alf's boyhood in Glasgow, his cousin Stan Wilkins from Sunderland came to visit, and to see the sights of Glasgow town. Alf recalled:

> ...in the afternoon we paid a visit to the art galleries and had a most enjoyable time. After that we had tea at Cranstons and then we popped into the Playhouse. We saw an excellent show and got home about ten o'clock.

Alf's day out says everything about the fine face of Glasgow and a great deal about the Wight family. The 'art galleries' were the Hunterian and the Kelvingrove, astride Kelvingrove Park. Aside from being two of the buildings that led John Betjeman (with his architecture-critic hat on) to describe Glasgow as 'the greatest Victorian city in Europe'), they also housed between them a world-class art collection. 'Cranstons' was a Glasgow institution, being one of the avant-garde 'art tea-rooms' of Miss Kate Cranston that she had decorated by Charles Rennie Mackintosh. Neil Munro (1863–1930), creator of 'Para Handy', was a journalist before he was a short-story writer. About Cranston's tea-rooms he wrote:

> They were deliberately conceived as houses of light refreshment most obviously for the pleasure of women and run wholly on 'temperance' lines...

Miss Cranston brought to light the genius of a Glasgow architect, Charles Mackintosh, who died only in recent years and was the inspiring influence of a group of Glasgow artists, men and women, who made her tea-rooms homogeneous in structure, decoration and furnishing. They were strangely beautiful the Cranston tea-rooms; women loved them, and 'Kate Cranstonish' became a term with Glasgow people in general to indicate domestic novelties in buildings and decorations not otherwise easy to define.

The top note in Miss Cranston's lunch-tea-room was struck by the one in Sauchiehall Street, which was popularly known as 'the room de luxe' from the chamber which was its most admired and exciting feature. There, even the cutlery and glassware had a character of their own, and thirty years ago no children's visit to the Circus was complete without a meal in this entrancing room de luxe, where everything was 'different' and the whole atmosphere was one of gay adventure.

Charles Rennie Mackintosh's 'Room de Luxe' for the Willow tea-rooms in Sauchiehall Street was inspired by a Rossetti poem, 'O, Ye, all ye that walk in Willow wood!'

A visit to art galleries, high tea at Kate Cranston's, an evening at the cinema. Only in dear old Glasgow town.

Taking tea at Kate Cranston's was also a middle-class rite of passage. Very few working-class people in Glasgow would have had either the money or the gall to visit such a bastion of the bourgeoisie. The Wights were socially aspirant. And, as parents, they also wanted the very best for Alf. Aspiration and devotion came together in their choice of secondary school for their much loved and only child.

Alf Wight left Yoker Primary in the summer of 1928. Nearly all his friends, among them Alex Taylor, went to the local state school, Victoria Drive Higher Grade School, but Alf went elsewhere. He had sat and passed the stiff entrance exams for Hillhead High School. A fee-paying co-educational school in the city's West End.

HILL TOPS

'I took the afternoon off [from school] and went to the
veterinary college for a consultation with the principal.
He said I would be O.K. going in without any Science
as they taught all that was necessary there.'

Alf Wight, diary, 28 April 1933

Alf Wight took the Corporation tram car across Glasgow to Hillhead High School on 3 September 1928; in more ways than one,
he was going up in the world. The Hillhead area in the West End
of Glasgow is aptly named. Geologically, it is a series of post-Ice
Age clay deposits forming a series of small hills or 'drumlins'. On
top of one of these drumlins sat Hillhead High School; from the
school's windows the view was all downhill to the flatness of the
Clyde riverside three miles away.

Hillhead was a shining example of the adage that the rich
people live on the hill; since the 1850s the area had been one of
Glasgow's most fashionable suburbs, following the exodus there of
the middle class from the inner-city's smoke and poverty. They went

westwards, as the better off did in every British city, to avoid the prevailing west to east wind blowing the diseases of the poor over them. By the turn of the nineteenth century, 80 per cent of Hillhead's residents were the professional classes, many of them employed in the neighbouring university; most of the rest of the inhabitants were their servants. To tempt the migrating bourgeoisie, canny property developers built honey sandstone tenements and terraces of Greco-Roman elegance; some of the tenement flats in Hillhead contained ten rooms. Visitors to the leafy streets and green spaces of Hillhead were reminded of Bath. Unlike roker, with its industrial din, Hillhead was a world of church quiet, interrupted only by the rustle of leaves and the occasional hansom horse cart. In Hillhead, children played in gardens; when they did play on the street, they did so in muted games of hopscotch and skipping to polite songs, such as Glaswegian William Miller's famous 'Wee Willie Winkie'.

Opening on Monday 13 April 1885, Hillhead High School stated its educational aspirations in stone. A forbidding four-storey building fronting Sardinia Terrace, Hillhead High School promised those about to pass through its gates (with separate gates for boys and girls) Calvinistic hard work; indeed, the building was built almost to the parameters of its street-corner plot, leaving small recreational space for its pupils. Inside, the building overran with austere classrooms, so many of them that headmasters numbered the rooms so that they, let alone the pupils, did not get lost. The school's motto was that of the Burg of Hillhead, *Je Maintiendrai* ('I Shall Maintain'), an oath promising to keep high standards of industry and discipline. But the grandiose Doric and Ionic classical columns on the building's façade, the portico, and the date of construction in Roman numerals – MDCCCLXXIV – advertised the importance the school attached to the making of gentlefolk. As the school's official history put it, the first headmaster, Mr Edward Macdonald, 'made his School a centre of learning; but he was still more intent on making it a building place of character, a training-ground for his pupils to fit themselves for the duties, responsibilities, and privileges of citizenship'.

Hillhead was self-consciously modelled on the English public schools and had accordingly suffered an extraordinary toll of its old boys in the Great War, only a decade before. In the axiom of the era, an officer was a gentleman who had attended a fee-paying school, and an officer had the most dangerous job in the trenches of the Western Front – leading the men over the top. No fewer than 178 Hillhead alumni had died in the 1914–18 conflict. The school's Officer Training Corps continued to be active, as were all the societies that public schools commonly enjoyed, from a debating society to a literary society to a drama club.

Sport was also an essential component in building the character that Edward Macdonald and successive heads wanted. Initially the cramped confines of the Sardinia Road site restricted sports to cycling and running – both of which could be done on Hillhead's roads – and Physical Training with moustachioed Colour-Sergeant William Walker, late of the Northumberland Fusiliers. The quintessential public and grammar schoolboy team games of rugby and cricket – soccer being regarded as suspiciously 'infra dig' in such circles – had to wait until the renting of a pitch at Glasgow Agricultural Society's showground at Scotstounhill.

Tucked away on the curriculum was the all-important lesson in the making of a gentleman: Elocution, twice a week. Later in life, Alf would refer to his own voice as 'glottal Clydeside'; maybe it was so when he first walked, wearing his cap, blazer and shorts, through Hillhead's boys' gate, but it wasn't when he left. It was a soft Scottish burr, refined at Hillhead. (Elocution lessons, unintentionally, did Alf the nascent writer a favour. By drawing an attentive ear to dialect, speech patterns and rhythms, it actually made them easier to reproduce. So when Alf transmogrified into James Herriot and wished to reproduce the dialogue of Yorkshire farmers and characters, he already had his ear in.)

In the Second City of Empire, only Glasgow High School rivalled Hillhead for its academic standards. A report by the Scottish Education Department in the summer of 1928 found that Hillhead's head of modern languages was 'outstanding', while the teaching of Latin was 'excellent' (a knowledge of the Classics being a *sine qua non* in the making of gentlemen and gentlewomen), Maths of 'a very high standard', and English 'thoroughly sound'.

Hillhead's list of literary luminescence did not end with Herriot. The future *Daily Express* editor Ian McColl – who 50 years later would serialize Herriot's books in his newspaper – was in the same class. Bestselling author Alistair Maclean also attended from 1937 to 1939. And perhaps a brighter star still in Hillhead's firmament was Robert W. Service, the 'Canadian Kipling' and the 'Bard of the Yukon', who had been a pupil in the 1880s. Service's 'The Shooting of Dan McGrew' is probably the best-selling poem of all time. Service wrote in his autobiography, *Ploughman of the Moon: An Adventure into Memory*, that 'At home it was a struggle to make frayed ends meet, yet each day we trooped off to what was then the Finest School in Scotland.' Forty years on, Alf Wight also set off to the fine school from a home worried by money. Most of the boys and girls were from very well-off homes on the doorstep, but there were others like Alf whose parents were hard pushed to pay the bill for the school on a hill.

It was quite a bill. When Alf started at Hillhead in 1928, the fees were £2-10s-0d a term; in April 1930 the fees were raised to £2-16s-0d a term so that the school could build up its clubs and societies. On top of the basic fees there was all the uniform, kit and caboodle to pay for: a boy's navy all wool blazer, with 'HHS' badge, cost 14/6d from Hoey's ('For Value') at 449 Dumbarton Road, or 18/6d for the tailor-made version; a cap with badge was 2/11d; the striped school tie 1/6d. If Alf's parents had been tempted to shop for school colours at Rowans on swish Buchanan Street, the prices were grimacingly expensive: a basic blazer was 21 shillings, a cap was 3/6, stockings (long socks to wear with shorts) were 2/6, a tie 2/6. A pair of 'Anniesland' rugby boots was 19/6d. In 1930, Alf's second year at Hillhead, his parents would have spent around £13 in fees, uniform and extras.

And this at a time when the Depression was raging. By April 1930, the number of shipyard workers on the Clyde had dropped to 29,000; in 1931 the most vivid proof of the Clyde's shipbuilding troubles came at John Brown's yard with suspension of work on the Cunard liner *Queen Mary*, the biggest ship in the world. A year later 125,819 people were unemployed in Glasgow. Porage and thin soup became the sole diet of thousands of the city's children, who would forever bear the mark of deprivation in stunted growth. But even those who had work found things tough; following the Wall Street Crash of 1929, the average wage for a 47 hour week for a tradesman in Britain fell to £2-4s-0d. Even when Pop was in work, he was earning less.

If the modesty of his Yoker background affected Alf Wight, he hid it well. Or, more likely, it simply did not bother him. Photographs of Alf in school uniform show a boy with an unfailing smile. In the privacy of his diary, Alf wrote about Hillhead: 'Of course school in some of its phases is an excrescence on the face of the earth – getting up at 7.45, homework, etc, but nevertheless there is something about it which makes it OK.' What made it OK? Larking with friends was one thing:

My face is pretty sore tonight having been the target for a great number of snowballs during the course of the day. During the dinner hour, we had a great scrap on the hill behind the school – the janitor, who is an officious wee man tried to stop us but retreated in disorder under a veritable barrage of snowballs. Oh, it was great to see him trying to be dignified and then beating it for dear life. I had a few skirmishes on the way to the car [tram] and I spent the evening trying to absorb a spot of knowledge in readiness for the forthcoming exams.

Then there was football at lunchtime. 'Our dinner-hour would be torture without our wee game of footer,' he told the diary. When the dreaded janitor stopped the playing of football at lunchtime because of a broken window, Alf bearded the lion in the den by going to the headmaster himself and asking permission to play. 'I got it and was a popular hero in consequence.'

Alf's enjoyment of school was doubtless aided by the fact that he was conspicuously clever. And what he didn't find easy, he worked at. Alf Wight, like his parents and grandparents, was a worker. 'There's no doubt about it – work is *the* thing to produce happiness,' he wrote in his diary. Placed in Form IC, Alf studied eight subjects in his first year: Science, Drawing, French, Maths, Latin, Geography, History and English. From the outset, Alf was markedly good at English, achieving 72 per cent in his end of year

exams, his best subject along with Latin. His second-year report
card described his progress as 'Very Good', a step up from the
'Good' of IC. He excelled at French, English and Latin – he later
mused that he read so much Virgil, Ovid and Cicero at home on
Dumbarton Road that he 'could have carried on an intelligent
conversation with an Ancient Roman'. In his Intermediate Certificate (the Scottish equivalent of modern GCSEs) at the end of
Form III, his performance was so outstanding that he was
declared the school's Intermediate Champion, the academic crème
de la crème.

Although James Herriot would unaffectedly describe himself as
'just a country vet', he long had an alter ego that was a wordsmith,
and at one early stage of his school life definitely harboured a desire
to be a journalist. He read ravenously: Sir Walter Scott, John
Buchan, H. G. Wells, Rider Haggard, G. A. Henty, and bought the
complete works of Milton from a book barrow in Renfield Street
for 'a bob'. Pop was smoking Kensitas cigarettes, and with the
coupons Alf sent off for a 14-volume set of Dickens in blue hard-
covers. With another 350 Kensitas coupons – in the style of the
time, Pop must have been smoking like a Clydebank chimney – Alf
secured the complete works of Shakespeare. Also on Alf's reading
list was American short-story writer O. Henry ('that man's a joy
to read'), Gothic detective novelist Wilkie Collins, and even
Thomas Macaulay, the highbrow Victorian essayist and historian.
He enjoyed Edgar Allan Poe, though only in small doses, because

too much Poe left him feeling depressed and morbid afterwards. ('I read some of Poe's queer, queer yarns. That chap must have spent all his time sitting thinking till his thoughts twisted themselves into strange shapes.') His indispensable reference source was *Arthur Mee's Children's Encyclopedia*; he kept his set of volumes all his life, and even read bits to his grandchildren. The books now sit on the shelves of the sitting room in The World of James Herriot museum in Thirsk, in the house that was the original for Skeldale.

But Alf's favourite author as boy and man was P. G. Wodehouse, the creator of Jeeves and Wooster. One doesn't need to be a Sherlock Holmes of the page to see some of the fingerprints of Alf Wight's boyhood reading on James Herriot's adult writing: the perfect narrative compression of O. Henry (the Herriot books being, if one cares to think about it, composed of loose-linked miniaturist autobiographical tales), and especially the comic heightening of character of Wodehouse. Both Siegfried and Tristan would be perfectly at home in a Wodehouse tale.

As a diarist, Alf was naturally enough interested in the master of the genre. After a visit to the public library at Whiteinch next to Yoker, Alf wrote in his journal:

While I was there [in the library] I saw a volume of Pepys' diary which interested me as I am emulating him through this tome. I think I'll begin each day with 'Up betimes and did go to the institution'.

Alf's diary was not the usual angsty teenage confessional or bare aide-memoire; it was like Pepys' journal – a full record of his life, particularly in 1933. He also *wrote* the diary, not kept it. Some of his enjoyment of words is evident in a note about 'school and its appurtenances':

> For English we have Mr Barclay ['Big Bill'] who is large, and at times, genial. I like him. For Latin we are in the care of Mr Buchanan ['Buckie'] whom I can't make much of. He is aged, tall, unhandsome and rather frail ... at times I think he's not bad and at times he gives me a pain in the neck. Mr Clark ['Brute Force'] who is small, dapper and likeable takes us for maths and Miss Chesters ['Soppy'] endeavours to pump French into us. Chesters is frank and almost boyish – I like her very well. Twice a week we get Mr ['Tarzan'] Brooks for Elocution. This bird, tho' probably well meaning is nothing but a funiosity.

Alf's 'elocuted' ear for speech is clear in his recording of Buckie's droning on about the need for the class to work harder for the Highers: 'Ah'm tellin' ye, ye've no go' a ghost o' a chance o' getting your Higher Latin – it takes students tae get it, no a lot' o' flibberty, gibberties like you.'

* * *

When Alf was 12, and still in his first year at Hillhead, there bounded into his life a character that would fix its course. Don was a Red Setter dog, given to Alf by his parents, partly as a reward for passing the entrance exam to the school. Although Alf already had pet cats in the apartment, a dog was different, more companionable than the solipsistic felines. However, as Alf found, the Red Setter (aka the Irish Setter) has certain drawbacks as a household pet, due to its gundog breeding. A genetic *pot pourri* of Irish Water Spaniel, Gordon Setter and Pointer, the Irish Red Setter was bred for brains and endurance, the latter quality requiring a lengthening of the leg. At 27 inches high and 70 lbs in weight, the Red Setter was a big dog for a small 'hoose' in a tenement. Worse, Don's intelligence combined with his desire for activity meant he quickly got bored. And when he got bored, he became destructive. More than once, Don caused mayhem in the apartment at 2172 Dumbarton Road. He also ran off. Often.

7/2/33: Don ran away tonight, the rascal, and hasn't returned – he'll be for it when he does.

15/2/33: Don ran away from mother tonight and has just arrived, very penitent and sorry for himself. He's a scream when he's in that condition – tail between his legs and rolling eyes – a picture of dejection.

21/2/33: I had to bath Don today as he ran away from Sadie and paid a visit to a particularly filthy field and returned smelling like a cow-bire.

For Alf these negatives of Don's were outweighed by the positives of the breed, which Don, 'lean, glossy and beautiful', had in abundance. Since Red Setters are used to close co-operation with humans, they are boundlessly affectionate, innately good-humoured and thoroughly responsive. A dog is a boy's best friend. Maybe especially so when it is a Red Setter.

On one occasion, at least, Don was put out to stud. Alf wrote in his diary on 12/2/33: 'Our Don has become the father of 11 thoroughbred Irish Setter puppies and so my reason for going to Hardgate was to see them. They were great wee things. Fat as barrels and squeaking away like anything.' Alf gave one of the pups to his friend Curly Marron, who lived in the same tenement block, and who had been a loyal companion on walks with Don. Curly christened the pup Rex. Soon after Rex became ill, teenage Alf dosed him with castor oil. This did little to cure Rex, and Curly's mother and sisters became terrified by the puppy's 'frequent outbursts' and wanted rid of him. Alf said the dog should see a vet. The vet said the illness would pass in a day or two. And, much to Alf and Curly's relief, it did. With Don at his heel, and sometimes Rex and Curly, sometimes with other friends and their dogs, Alf walked along the canal, along the 'Boulevarde' (Dumbarton Road), but also regularly tramped out into the countryside at the top of Kelso Street.

There were expeditions further afield too. 'Living in the extreme west where the city sprawl thinned out into the countryside,' Alf recalled in James Herriot's Dog Stories, 'I could look from my windows on to the Kilpatrick Hills and Campsie Fells in the north and over the Clyde to Neilston Pad and the hills beyond Barrhead to the south. Those green hills beckoned to me and though they were far away, I walked to them.' Those green hills were at least 15 miles away but he walked to them often. 'I spent the whole day,' he wrote on 25 June 1933, 'in a tramp to the Whangie & over the O.K. hills with Jimmy [Turnbull] & Jock Davy. It was simply wonderful.'

On the repeated road to the hills, Alf had a change of perspective. Hitherto he had been a city boy. Somewhere in those green remembered hills around Glasgow, he became a country lover.

Something else happened to Alf out in the scented, intoxicating Lanarkshire hills. Watching Don and the other dogs romp and run, Alf realized that he was intrigued by the behaviour of canines – and that he wanted to work with dogs, rather than with words. He did not abandon writing, but the animals began trumping the words.

The light-bulb moment came when Alf was 15 (he tended to misremember it as 13), when he read an article in Meccano Magazine's 'What Shall I Be?' series entitled 'No. XXVI – A

VETERINARY SURGEON', by G. P. Male, President of the Royal College of Veterinary Surgeons, in December 1931. Male wrote:

> *Veterinary surgery is one of the few professions in which the number of entrants has shown a considerable decline in recent years. This decline is probably due to the belief that the expansion of motor traffic and similar changes have reduced the prospect of success in the profession. The belief is a mistaken one, however, for the decline in the importance of the horse is being at least partially counteracted by a growing demand for the services of the veterinary surgeon in other directions. The prospects of those now entering this comparatively neglected profession are bright, particularly if they approach it with a real liking for animals and for the open-air life that it entails.*

As Alf read, he 'felt a surging conviction' that veterinary medicine was the career for him. 'As a vet, I could be with dogs all the time, attending to them, curing their illnesses, saving their lives.' The conviction that his destiny was to become a dog doctor was cemented by a visit to Hillhead High from Dr A. W. Whitehouse, the principal of Glasgow Veterinary College. Like Male, 'Old Doc' Whitehouse refused to believe that the veterinary profession was on its last legs because of the motor car and the tractor, and went to Hillhead as a convinced recruiter for his occupation in general, his college in particular. He told the assembled pupils, Alf recalled later, 'If you decide to become a veterinary surgeon you will never grow rich but you will have a life of endless interest and variety.'

One boy, at least, was persuaded by Dr Whitehouse's evangelizing. Henceforth, Alf Wight knew exactly what he wanted to do with his life. But the obstacles, he realized, were enormous. Veterinary science was, well, science, and Alf Wight was, in his own words, 'certainly not a scientific type'. He had already chosen to specialize in Arts subjects over science at school, and with his 'Highers', the Scottish equivalent of A-levels, already on the horizon he could not swap midstream. So the 15-year-old Alf Wight went up to Glasgow Veterinary College on Buccleuch Street to seek Dr Whitehouse's advice. Years later he wrote:

He listened patiently as I poured out my problems.

'I love dogs,' I told him. 'I want to work with them. I want to be a vet. But the subjects I am taking at school are English, French and Latin. No science at all. Can I get into the college?'

He smiled. 'Of course you can. If you get two higher and two lowers you have the matriculation standard. It doesn't matter what the subjects are. You can do Physics, Chemistry and Biology in your first year.'

But one anxiety still gnawed away. Alf Wight was poor at Maths. Would he, he asked Dr Whitehouse, need Maths to be a vet? The old veterinarian laughed, and replied, 'Only to add up your day's takings.'

* * *

With his career goal set, Alf Wight worked harder still at school. With the tutoring and encouragement of English master 'Johnny' Gibb, Alf counted among his triumphs in the fourth form the winning of the prize for English. A poem, authored by Alf and 'DMM', appeared in the December 1932 issue of the school magazine. Entitled 'Four o'clock', the poem is a parody of Thomas Gray's *Elegy Written in a Country Churchyard* from 1751:

The buzzing bell doth screech the ended day,
The toil-worn herd winds slowly home to tea;
The teachers homewards wend their weary way,
And leave the School to 'jannies' big and wee.

Now fades the fog-bound landscape from the sight,
And all the School a solemn stillness holds,
Save where the cleaners sweep with all their might
And clanging pail the hidden dirt enfolds.

Save that from yonder smoothly swinging doors
The moping 'jan' doth audibly complain

To such as playing football after hours,
Infest his all too desolate domain.

The icy blast of cold and frosty morn,
The ringing of alarms beside their head,
The milk-boy's skirl, the matutinal horn
Will tear them, on the morrow, from their bed.

Six months later, another poem by 'JAW' appeared in the *Hillhead High School Magazine*: this time the target of the schoolboy spoofing is Hamlet's 'Angels and ministers of grace defend us!' soliloquy, spoken by the prince when he first sees the ghost – and calls upon all things holy to protect him:

Angels and ministers of grace defend us!
Be thou a verb, a noun, an adjective,
Come thou from Virgil, Livy, Cicero
Thy object, or to help or hinder me—
Thou comest in such a questionable shape
That I will guess at thee: I'll call thee Noun,
Pronoun, Conjunction – anything! Oh! Answer me!
Let me not burst in ignorance; but tell
Why the examiners, fiend e'en though they be
Do thus maltreat me; why the dictionary,
In which thou hast been quietly inurn'd

Hath ope'd his ponderous and gilt-edged jaws
To cast thee up at me. What may this mean
That thou, foul word, so tangled, and unreal,
Revisit'st thus the examination room,
Making day hideous; and me befooled,
So horridly to shake my disposition
With thoughts beyond the reaches of my soul?
Say, why is this? Wherefore? What should I do?

Ironically, it was Alf's very ability at English that led him into trouble at school. For three years, his Maths master, Mr Filshie, had tolerantly shrugged his shoulders at Alf's regrettable mathematics, the nadir being 5 per cent in a trigonometry exam. When Alf won the Intermediate prize, followed by the English prize, Filshie suddenly woke up to the fact that Alf Wight was a very bright boy. 'Wight,' Filshie boomed one day, 'I have always thought you were just an amiable idiot and have treated you accordingly, but now I see that you have come out top of the class in your English paper, so I can only conclude that you have not been trying for me. Hold out your hands.' Six of the best on Alf's palms followed. (Unlike English schools, which used the cane for punishment, the leather strap or 'Lochgelly tawse' was the common means of inflicting corporal punishment north of the border.)

By 1932, Hillhead High School had moved from its pinched confines at Sardinia Terrace (since renamed Cecil Street: the old school building now houses Hillhead Primary) to a new site three streets away on Oakfield Avenue. So popular had the school become that the governors' constant sub-dividing of rooms was no longer a solution acceptable to the Education Department, which threatened to take away the school's grant. Given Hillhead High School's social aspirations, it must have pleased the governors no end that the Oakfield address lay opposite Eton Terrace, which had been designed by one of Glasgow's greatest Victorian architects, Alexander 'Greek' Thomson. Thomson, for his part, probably revolved in his grave as the new Hillhead High rose from the mud of the drumlin. In the reverse of the usual construction industry scenario, the school cost *less* than the estimate (by half, of a given figure of £183,000) and the budget for architects Messrs. Wylie, Shanks and Wylie must have been particularly skimped on. With its awkward back-to-back Y shape and its red bricks, Hillhead High School hardly boasted perfect Classical proportions. Still, when the 736 senior pupils moved in on 1 September 1931 they most likely marvelled at the echoing spaces of the two gymnasia, the hall with a stage, the art rooms, laboratories, library and refectory. However, despite the change in location and the greater space, the round of school life continued as before: there was the Armistice Day service in Belmont Church, the march past the War Memorial on the first school day after Remembrance Sunday, the Christmas holiday, 'skating' days off when it was really icy, the holiday on 26 May to celebrate King George V's birthday, the annual summer garden party and half holiday in June, the end of year speech day in the Woodside Hall in July, cricket in summer, rugby in winter…

Sport was one of the aspects of school that made it rather more than 'OK' for Alf. He had a medal to hang around his neck for coming second in the Inter-Scholastic sports under-16 broad jump, and in his final year his prowess with a cat-gut racket saw him in the school tennis final. He also made the rugby Second XV. Hillhead was a die-hard rugby school, and during Alf's time there it contained a clutch of boys who would go on to play club rugby, even to represent Scotland in the sport of the oval ball. Alas, Hillhead Second XV endured a string of defeats caused by a phenomenon known to every schoolboy rugger player. On losing to Kilmarnock High, Alf entered in his diary: 'We were beaten but not disgraced as the other team was made of huge bruisers – six footers to a man.' Another match: 'I'm sorry to have to say we were beaten this morning and no wonder, as the Shawlands chaps were six footers to a man.'

When not in school, Alf's life as a teenager was, like his life as a small boy, a round of hobbies, of making stuff and doing things. Since television was in its infancy and only available in one house in a thousand until the late 1930s, the only 'on tap' entertainment in the home was the radio. The first Scottish studio of the BBC opened up at 202 Bath Street in 1923, and making crystal radios to receive transmissions became a mad craze, much to the annoyance of the General Post Office (GPO) because hundreds of

Glaswegians stole the earpieces from public phone boxes for their home radio sets.

The Twenties and Thirties are thought of as the hobbies decades for good reason: the school-leaving age had been raised to 14. To help children – and the children's parents – pass all the weekends and holidays of the school year, publishers galore issued comics and tomes with advice on rewarding hobbies. *Modern Wonders for Boys*, a book published by Glasgow's The Sunshine Press in the mid-Thirties was typical of the ilk, with articles on painting on glass, simple apparatus for the amateur conjurer, photography, stamp collecting, poker work, DIY winter decorations, making a bookshelf (there were legions of boys knocking up bookshelves in the Thirties, among them J. Wight, junior), getting the best out of cricket, as well as, ambitiously, 'How to Make a Simple Canvas Canoe'.

But hobby books were about more than time-filling, they were regarded as tools for education, thus were peppered with general knowledge articles. *Modern Wonders* contained informative pieces on aeroplanes (always a winner with Thirties boys), clocks, the Seven Wonders of the World, glass-blowing in Venice, hoovers, electro-magnets, ships through the ages, signalling, submarines, X-rays, wild ponies of Britain, spiders, newspaper presses, coal mining … To sugar the educative pill, *Modern Wonders* filled the intervals with breathless fictional tales of derring-do (explorer Professor Ward in 'The Last of the Lizards') and schoolboys having wholesome fresh air adventures tackling foreign spies.

Save for not tackling dinosaurs and thick-accented German agents, Alf managed a full gamut of pastimes. He took Don for a walk every day, often twice a day ('Of course Don and I took our inevitable constitutional'), he kicked the round ball around with friends in the park, went with his mother to see Rachmaninov in concert (Alf remembered that he looked like a 'big bear' huddled over the keyboard), tried conjuring, juggling ('the house has resonated with the sound of falling balls tonight'), tried muscle-building with chest-expanders and hand-squeezers, joined Yoker Tennis Club, watched Rangers, watched Celtic, watched Yoker Athletic, had a notion to read the Bible (for the meaning and the beauty of the words), took up hitting the 'wee white ball' with a club ('In the morning, I played golf. In the afternoon, I played golf. In the evening, I played golf'), trained in various athletics disciplines (hurdles, javelin, discus) and took up fretwork. He carried on 'piano-walloping', albeit informally, being inspired by the new music coming in from America.

I've taken a notion to make myself a good jazz pianist as hitherto I've only played straight stuff. I think I'll send to Uncle Bob [in Sunderland] and ask him for a loan of his book on jazz playing.

Alf's Sunderland relatives also kept him liberally supplied with the local newspapers so he could follow the fortunes of Sunderland AFC, with their exultant highs:

28 January 1933: *Oh boy, oh boy! What a day! Why weren't these spaces made bigger.* **Sunderland have defeated Aston Villa, by three goals to nothing at Villa Park!** *Aston Villa, the greatest cup-fighting team in England, the team whose name is a household word and whose traditions are more glorious than any other club in England. And Sunderland, who had met them umpteen times before in the cup without success, licked them!*

And their inevitable lows:

8 March 1933: *Eheu! I am plunged into the very depths of despondency. Life to me dark and gloomy and the future looms up, forbidding and hopeless – Sunderland have been defeated by Derby County at Roker Park in the cup-tie before the semi-final … Oh, it is sickening!*

There was also going to the cinema. Since Pop was still playing piano in the intervals at cinemas, Alf got complimentary tickets, particularly for the 2000-seat art deco Commodore at 1297 Dumbarton Road, which opened on Boxing Day 1932. The programme for the first evening, attended by the Wights, was:

Our Managing Director, Mr GEORGE SINGLETON,
has a few words to say.

* * * * * * * *

PARAMOUNT NEWS – A Pictorial Review of Daily Events

* * * * * * * *

MICKEY'S ORPHANS – Mickey Mouse at it Again!

* * * * * * * *

PATHETONE WEEKLY – To interest, to educate and to amuse

* * * * * * * *

SLIPPERY PEARLS

A real novelty with over twenty well-known artistes in the cast including Laurel and Hardy; Wheeler and Woolsey; Joe E. Brown; Buster
Keaton; Norma Shearer; Joan Crawford; William Beery; etc

* * * * * * * *

THEN and NOW

Remember the good old days? This is the kind of film we used to enter-
tain you with around 1912 and the musical (?) accompaniment is as
near to the real thing as we care to remember.

* * * * * * * *

MESSRS. PARAMOUNT FILM SERVICE LTD.
PRESENTS
MARLENE DIETRICH: CLIVE BROOK
Supported by
Anna May Wong: Warner Oland
And Eugene Pallette

In

THE SHANGHAI EXPRESS
Based on the story by Harry Hervey.
Directed by Josef von Sternberg
'A' Certificate

There were continuous performances each evening from 6.15 until 10.45, and on Saturday from 2.30 until 11 pm. In the manner of the medieval London apprentices who were fed so much salmon that they tired of the luxury, Alf surfeited on cinema, writing in his diary: 'Oh! Pictures again.' He didn't like *Grand Hotel* with Greta Garbo, who he thought should be 'put in a lunatic asylum and kept under close observation'. Otherwise, 1933 was a good year for the movies: Popeye made his spinach-slurping bow, the Marx Brothers were in *Duck Soup,* Laurel and Hardy pretended to be *Sons of the Desert*, and Mae West put her best chest forward in *She Done Him Wrong* and *I'm No Angel,* both with Cary Grant. But even Glaswegians without 'comp' tickets went to the cinema, on average three times a week; everywhere else in Britain, the average was once a fortnight. The warmth of the cinema, and that touch of luxury in a hard life, was no doubt as big a draw as the escapism shown on the silver screen.

Just after his fourteenth birthday Alf asked a girl out to the cinema; on the way into Glasgow on the tram, he asked for a penny ticket and handed over a half-crown piece (2/6d). Annoyed at being given so large a coin for so small a fare, the conductor took revenge by giving Alf the change in 58 halfpennies. This left Alf at the cinema kiosk, to his red-faced embarrassment, laboriously counting out the two shillings for the tickets in the conductor's ha'pennies, thus holding up the queue. Alf claimed that it was four excruciating years before he plucked up the courage to ask another girl for a date. And so, thwarted in puppy love, Alf was back to hanging around with his mates.

Like many of his Yoker friends, Alf was a member of the Boys' Brigade, then in its heyday. The Boys' Brigade was formed in Glasgow in 1883, when William Alexander Smith surveyed his pubescent unruly pupils at the Sabbath School of the Free College Church in Hillhead. About to finally despair of his inability to interest or control the class, Smith had a notion: He was also an officer in the 1st Lanarkshire Rifle Volunteers, so why not use military methods (principally drill and discipline) and values (obedience and self-respect) to run the church Sunday youth club? As Smith expressed it later, his object was 'the advancement of Christ's Kingdom among boys and the promotion of habits of Reverence, Discipline, Self-Respect, and all that tends towards a true Christian Manliness'.

The Free College Church's minister, Reverend George Reith, gave his enthusiastic backing. (Reith was the father of John Reith, who became the first Director-General of the BBC – thus Glasgow gave the world the inventor of the television in John Logie Baird, the overseer of television's most famous station, and the creator of one of television's most successful series.)

Realizing that a full uniform would be beyond the pockets of most of the boys' parents, Smith developed an 18d outfit of a 'pill box' forage cap, a belt, a haversack and a badge, on which was struck an anchor and the motto 'Sure and Steadfast', taken from Epistles to the Hebrews, chapter 6, verse 19 ('Which hope we have as an anchor of the soul, both sure and steadfast'). In this minimalist uniform, Smith's volunteers drilled, prayed, sung hymns and studied the Bible each Sunday at the Woodside Road Mission Hall. In pursuit of the 'manliness' in 'Christian manliness', Smith arranged swimming sessions, cricket, gymnastics with dumbbells and Indian clubs. It was intrinsic to the age that a healthy body and healthy mind were symbiotic. A Club Room supplied board games, religious readings, as well as Boy's Own classics, many of them supplied free by Glasgow publisher Blackie and Son, including *Kidnapped*, *The Black Arrow* and *Ben-Hur*.

Fifty-nine boy volunteers attended the inaugural parade of the 1st Glasgow Company of The Boys' Brigade on 4 October 1883. Some 20 dropped out when it became clear that Smith was a stickler for discipline – any boy even a minute late for 8 am parade was not allowed to 'fall in' – but the Boys' Brigade became a wild success in that sector of Glasgow working-class society that believed most soberly in 'getting on'. People like the Wights of Dumbarton Road.

One of the prime attractions of the 'BB' for boys was the annual summer camp in the same week as Glasgow's Fair Holiday, when the entire city's heavy industry shut down for the duration. The general routine for the day, which did not change for decades, was:

6.00 am   *Reveille*

7.00 am   *Bathing parade (Boats) and service of biscuits*

9.00 am	First Breakfast Bugle
9.15 am	Breakfast
9.45 am	Morning Prayers
10.45 am	Dress Bugle
11.00 am	Inspection of Camp and Full-Dress Parade
1.15 pm	First Dinner Bugle
1.30 pm	Dinner
5.45 pm	First Tea Bugle
6.00 pm	Tea
7.00 pm	Fishing Parade (Boats)
9.30 pm	Evening Prayers
9.45 pm	Tattoo
10.00 pm	Lights Out

In between the parades and prayers, there was plenty of time for sport and recreation. BB camps were one of the places that Alf improved the backhand that allowed him in his twenties, armed with a Slazenger tennis racket, to reach the West of Scotland men's doubles final with his partner Colin Kesson.

By 1933, the Brigade's jubilee year, the movement had spread across Britain and the globe; in Britain alone 111,871 British boys were enrolled, plus 52,219 in the associated Life Boys. The Brigade's jubilee Conventicle, held at Hampden Park, was the largest open-air service held in Britain, with 130,000 inside the stadium, and 100,000 without. The sun shone all day.

For many city boys, the 'BB' summer camp, which was usually at Loch Fyne or North Berwick, was their one and only holiday. Not for Alf Wight. At Easter 1933 he attended a camp organized by Yoker church's Sunday Club (at which an inspiring speech by the commandant left him and his friends 'with a new determination to be decent fellows to the best of our ability') and during the summer he enjoyed a holiday at West Kilbride, staying alone with friends of the family. After several days purely in the company of Dorothy Ash and Evelynne Sorley, Alf's diary is filled with Wodehousian comic detail:

18 July:

Allah be praised! This afternoon, Dorothy introduced me to a lad by the name of Monty Gilbert – he seems a decent spud. We went down for a bathe immediately. He's interested in all the things I like – sport, athletics, physical culture, and besides can talk seriously too. If I hadn't met him, I'm sure my reason would have broken down under the strain of gallivanting around with a couple of females.

19 July:

In the morning, Monty and I had a glorious swim and sunbathe down at Ardneil Bay. It was the life. In the afternoon, we went into Saltcoats for a swim in the pool. There we met Do [orothy] and went afterwards to Mrs Duncan's house for tea. After tea, we went into the drawing room to see Mr Duncan's cine-kodak films. One of them, which was taken last year, showed Dorothy acting the goat. It was a scream and Monty and I just lay back and howled...

Friday 21:

Another day of sunbathing and swimming, very like yesterday. Monty is a great lad. I wish he lived in Glasgow for I believe he's the sort of fella I'd like for a friend. David Sommerville seems to be cracked over Evelynne, the poor fish; he mopes about and can't go anywhere without her. He's the laughing-stock of the place, and I believe he knows it. I was at a garden party with Do. And I won the tennis tournament. Beat Dorothy in the final – it took me all my time too. D. Also won the treasure hunt, so we more or less cleared the board between us.

Tuesday 25:

Knocked out of the [tennis] tournament alas! I was beaten 6-3 – anyway I've nothing to bother me now. I bathed with Monty in the afternoon. I had the usual evening – a walk and then listened to the wireless. I haven't much to say tonight so I'll conclude the entry with a few remarks on various people. Evelynne has dropped down to zero in my estimation as I have found she is a tale-bearing, petty and deceitful little wretch. In short, a nasty bit of work. As to Dorothy, although she exasperates and irritates me terribly with her headstrong childish ways, she appears to be very straight and open. So Monty and I regard her as a fairly decent spud.

Friday 28:
The weather was a treat so the 'gang' spent morning and afternoon at Ardneil Bay. It was marvellous! In the evening Monty and I went to Saltcoats and visited a cinema. We saw a really first-class show – a British picture called 'Sherlock Holmes'. We had a good blether on the road home.

After nearly three weeks at West Kilbride, Alf's mother, father and Don came to take him home to Dumbarton Road. There he suffered 'a holiday ache', a nostalgia for West Kilbride. But not for long; a day later, he went with his parents to Sunderland for the marriage of his cousin Stan Wilkins. (Sunderland, incidentally, offered more than kin to the Wights; the Roker and Fullwell areas were the seaside, bathers and cafes, sand and hot pies, and the Wights often holidayed there.) After Sunderland, Alf was off with his mother to Arran on the Firth of Clyde, where well-to-do Glasgow liked to spend the summer, before attending the BB camp at Loch Fyne. And then back to West Kilbride.

But Alf's life was not all one long holiday.

* * *

The year before, 1932, Alf had contracted diphtheria. One reason for the sheer exhilaration he felt – and communicated in his diary – on his holiday in 1933 was the sheer relief of being alive.

Caused by the bacteria *Corynebacterium diphtheria,* the disease produces a grey film (*diphtheria* is Greek for 'a piece of leather') that can block the airways. Meanwhile, the toxins produced by the bacteria produce skin boils and lesions, as well as infiltrate the bloodstream to reach the organs.

Queen Victoria's daughter Alice and granddaughter Marie of Hesse both died from diphtheria, but it is mainly a disease of the crowded city street, not the spacious palace, because it is spread by droplets. Tenement Glasgow, with the highest population density in Western Europe, bred diphtheria as though it was some maniacal laboratory; during the period 1934–42 alone, 1210 Glaswegians died from the disease. Alf suffered from diphtheria abscesses over his body for two years after contracting the disease.

Inevitably, the brush with death affected Alf. His decision, whether taken consciously or unconsciously, to keep a diary in 1933 was a life-affirming gesture, a young boy's bid for immortality. His natural enthusiasm for life was increased; a prime new enthusiasm, unsurprisingly, was keeping fit. Along with many a boy in the 1930s, he turned to Lieutenant J. P. Muller for guidance on how to keep the body beautiful and healthy.

The name of Jurgen Peter Muller is now forgotten, but before the Second World War he was a major – and perfectly toned –

figure on the cultural landscape of Europe. (The principal of Glasgow School of Art, where Muller appeared during a lecture tour in 1911, declared Muller's body the most perfect he had ever seen.) Born in 1866 in Asserballe, Denmark, Muller had been so small as a baby that 'I could be placed in an ordinary cigar box'. He almost died of dysentery at two and 'contracted every childhood complaint' thereafter. During his teens, however, he improved his health by a strict regimen of exercises. In other words, he triumphed over puniness and sickliness by his own efforts, and not by the benefit of inherited genes. Eventually, in 1904, Muller put down his regimen in words. With its distinctive cover picture of Apoxyomenos, the Greek athlete, naked and towelling himself, *My System: 15 Minutes' Exercise a Day for Health's Sake* went on to sell 2 million copies and to be translated into 25 languages. Muller himself eventually settled in London, where he opened the Muller Institute at 45 Dover Street and dropped the umlaut from his name in order to make it seem less German. Business boomed. The Prince of Wales gave Muller his official imprimatur, the British Army adopted his fitness regime, and Muller added to his catalogue with *My System for Women*, *My System for Children*, *My System of Breathing*, *The Daily Five Minutes* and *My Sunbathing and Fresh Air System*, among others. The cult of 'Mullerism' swept Europe, and the man himself became the Dane more famous than Hans Christian Andersen. In recognition of his services to physical health (and to raising Denmark's international profile) the King of

Denmark conferred a knighthood of the Order of the Dannebrog on Muller.

'Why be weakly?' asked *My System*, before answering with a regimen that involved a suitable diet, sensible underclothes (less was best, contra the Victorian fashion for corsets), moderate indoor temperatures, eight hours' sleep a night, and a quarter of an hour of exercises daily. These exercises were preferably undertaken whilst wearing few clothes and deep-breathing fresh air (outdoors or in front of an open window were the best locations for the System). The first eight exercises advocated by Muller were essentially gymnastic or balletic stretches, including Slow Trunk-Circling, Quick Leg-Swinging, Quick Arm-Raising, and were ended with a cold bath and a vigorous towelling. Then followed ten exercises of muscular stretching whilst simultaneously rubbing the body. Muller wrote:

> *The rubbing is done with the palms of the hands, and should be a simple stroking or friction to begin with; later on, as one's strength increases, it should be so vigorous that it becomes a sort of massage ... After you have followed up my System for some time, the skin will assume quite a different character; it will become firm and elastic, yet as soft as velvet and free from pimples, blotches, spots or other disfigurements.*

Like other early twentieth-century physical culturalists such as Joseph Pilates, Muller believed that his gymnastic exercises had definite medical benefits and could treat everything from acidity to writer's cramp, including the devastations of old age. In an era of rampant infection, Muller's insistence that anybody could best disease by exercise, fresh air and sunlight was engaging. Before antibiotics, Muller's prescription for fresh air was one of the few preventative measures people could take to ward off TB. (Muller had once worked as an inspector at the Vejlefjord Tuberculosis Sanitorium and he went on to become one of Denmark's leading athletes.) But there was more to Muller's system than mere physicality; philosophically, it was aimed at the individual and was open to anybody. In an age of rampant political extremism, other gymnastic movements were tinged with nationalist or Communist tones. The Muller method needed neither expensive equipment nor membership of a political organization. Other 'Mullerists' included the arch-individualist of the twentieth century, Franz Kafka.

Alf Wight did his Muller regime even on school mornings in winter:

Diary, 9/1/33:
Back to the old school routine again. Up at 7.45. BRR!
Exercises and cold bath and a final exhilarating dash after
my car [tram].

Diary, 12/1/33:

It took a bit of willpower to get me into the cold bath this morning as it was cold enough to freeze the whiskers off a monkey.

It was also too cold, Don decided, to leave the kitchen couch. After months of 'Mullering', however, Alf was able to report in his diary on 20 April 1933:

I'm feeling as fit as the proverbial fiddle. I put it all down to the exercises and cold baths. I am much brighter and healthier than I was last year before my illness and I seem to be on the upgrade.

He also 'set down my figures' in his diary with the intention of improving on them:

Height: 5 ft, 8¾ [*Would like to get a bit taller*]

Weight: 10 stone 2 lbs [*not bad*]

Chest: 34 ins (normal) 35¾ (expanded) [*Room for improvement*]

Biceps: 11 ins [*my arms are my poorest part*]

Forearm: 10 ½ ins [*don't know if I'm in the right [word indistinct]*]

Neck: 14 ins [*decent*]

Waist:	*27½ [Should I have pulled it in?]*
Calf:	*14 ins*
Wrists:	*6½ [awful!]*

He thought the diphtheria cost him a place in the rugby first XV, but there was always summer sports to shine at, and he decided that 'I am going to enter everything within my scope at sports day, that is, the 100 yards, 220 yards, broad jump ... discus, javelin, hurdles, cricket-ball, and place and drop kick. I'm leaving the long distances alone.'

A certain McKechnie was slated to win everything, but Alf decided 'I am going to do something about it. I used to be able to beat him in the 100 yards and last year I did 19 ft. in the long jump so I start training tomorrow, full of hope.' A pulled muscle put paid to Alf's intended track and field glories, but he kept up the Muller regime for years. When his own son, Jim Wight, went to Glasgow veterinary school, he gave him a copy of *My System*.

Alf's illness affected his academic performance at school – he lost more than a month of lessons in the Michaelmas (autumn) 1932 term – but fortunately only by degree, not by kind. His final marks on his record card show 'Eng. 67, Hist. 52, Latin 48, French 53, Maths 40' and in the 'School Honours' column his award of 'Leaving Cert [ificate]' is noted. Alf Wight left Hillhead High on 30 June 1933 with Higher Passes in English, Latin and French and Lower passes in History and, miraculously, even Maths. He wrote in his diary:

What a day! What a day! I awoke this morning a poverty-stricken youth, and am going to bed a rich man. This morning, we had the prize-giving and I got 4/6d for being runner-up in the championship and then took my departure from Hillhead, and all the pleasant things connected with it but on the other hand, I'm glad to have got my higher at the age of 16 yrs and 8 months and to be able to get on with my job. I'll join the F.P. [Former Pupils] Club of course, and keep up my connection with the school. In the evening, Curly and I went to the Commodore with the complimentary ticket, and saw an excellent programme. Afterwards, Mother presented me with ten bob for getting my highers.

His parents must have believed that their efforts had been worth it. As always he had been a model pupil, and was marked 'Ex[cellent]' in Progress, Diligence and Conduct.

His report card also clearly noted Alf's reason for leaving.

'Gone to Veterinary College.'

ALL THINGS UNWISE AND WONDERFUL

'Keep the animal's bowels open and trust to God.'

Lecturer, Glasgow Veterinary College

The profession of veterinary surgeon may not be the world's oldest, but the first domesticators of the dog, cow and horse undoubtedly had sages who took some form of medical care of their fur-coated charges, if only to pick out thorns from paws and stones from hooves. The practice of veterinary medicine was documented throughout the Ancient World: Chinese records from 4000 BC note the use of herbs for the healing of livestock; the Egyptian Papyri of Kahun (1900 BC) contain excerpts of a textbook detailing animal anatomy and diseases; a century later the Indians had veterinary hospitals; circa 1750 BC the legal Code of King Hammurabi of Mesopotamia listed a scale of fees for treatment of asses and oxen; both Hippocrates and Aristotle in Ancient Greece wrote about the treatments of sick animals; Urlagaldinna in Mesopotamia made a deliberate study of animal healing in about 300 BC, leading some to claim him as 'The World's First Veterinary Surgeon'.

But it was under the Romans that the practice of veterinary medicine became commonplace. After all, the stocks-in-trade of the Romans were farming and warring, and both required animals. The Latin for 'animal doctor' was *veterinarius*, as patented by Columella, who wrote 12 volumes on agriculture and animal husbandry circa AD 42–68. (His treatment for scab in sheep was olive oil.) Prescriptions by Roman wise men like Columella and Cato would be used in farmyards until medieval times.

Veterinary medicine, though, has mainly evolved from the treatment of the occupant of the Roman stable, not farmyard. In Ancient Rome the farrier was the most important animal healer; the all-conquering Roman Army required vast numbers of horses, and to ensure their battle-readiness, the farrier not only shod *equii* but maintained their health by following equine welfare codes. The glory that was Roman veterinary science was crowned by the publication of Vegetius' *Books of the Veterinary Art* in AD 450.

When the Western Roman Empire fell to the barbarians in 476, veterinary medicine entered a Dark Age. Although the countryside of Europe swarmed with self-proclaimed animal healers, from 'cow-leeches' (who tended sheep as well as bovines) to 'hog-gelders', the standard of their practice was epitomized by a medieval cure for constipation in oxen:

A lively trout … was taken from the adjoining stream, and committed to the gullet of the patient, under the assurance

that it would soon work its way through all impediments,
and speedy relief be afforded.

Neither the ox nor the fish survived. But no matter because, ultimately, survivals of beasts, like humans, was a matter for God. If the cow-leech or God failed, spells, astrology and charms were invoked.

The most fortunate beasts in medieval times were those left untreated, because their peers were purged, bled, fired – or stuffed with trout – before dying. What useful knowledge did survive the Dark Ages, from effective herbs to observations on animal behaviour, was in the hands of apprenticeship-serving farriers, or 'marshals' as they were known in the time of chivalry.

It took more than a thousand years to pass from Vegetius' *Veterinary Art* to the next significant landmark in veterinary science. In 1598 *Anatomia Del Cavallo* ('The Anatomy of the Horse') by the late Bolognese aristocrat Carlo Ruini left the printers, with startlingly detailed and accurate woodcuts of equine anatomy. A few years later, in 1610, *Markham's Master-Peece, or, What doth a Horse-man lacke* by Englishman Gervase Markham, appeared, providing hundreds of cures for illnesses both 'physicall and chirugicall', including descriptions of medications 'which of mine owne knowledge I know to be certaine and most approved'.

Markham's book is typical in what was wrong – and right – with veterinary medicine at the time. A former soldier, the first person to import an Arabian horse into England, the champion of improved horse-breeding, Markham was neither fool nor fraudster. With 50 years' experience in the 'Horse-leech-craft', he could with some accuracy detect what was wrong with an animal by observation – from its gait, its poise, its dung.

Where Markham's knowledge failed him was in the workings of an animal's body, which he held, like centuries of farriers and marshals before him, to be determined by ethereal, spirit-like 'humours' and 'temperaments'.

Markham's book was a fixture in the library of the world's first veterinary school, which was founded in Lyons, France, in 1762 by M. Claude Bourgelat, director of the city's *Academie Royale d'Equitation*. Bourgelat was an Enlightenment rationalist who believed that medicine should be based on observation and experimentation. He was also an *ecuyer*, a master of horses, who ensured that the syllabus of the *ecole veterinaire* concentrated heavily on equine matters. The students Bourgelat sought for his enterprise were 'ordinary farriers', and the only requirement for admission to the new school was the ability to read and write, evidence of baptism and a certificate of good conduct. There was no lower age limit; in 1762, an 11-year-old child was in the same class as a 30-year-old man.

The horse would dominate the teaching of veterinary science until the 1930s, when Alf Wight was at Glasgow Veterinary College, for reasons both good and bad.

RIGHT: Hannah Bell, Alf's mother.

BELOW: Hannah Wight (née Bell) in later life; as well as being an accomplished singer, she ran a thriving dress-making business.

LEFT: James Henry Wight, Alf's father, ship plater and musician.

BELOW: The Wights on their wedding day; Sergeant Alfred Wight, after whom Alf was named, is bottom left. He was killed in the battle of the Somme.

ABOVE: Shipyards on the river Wear in Sunderland, Alf's place of birth, and where James Wight made his living. The photo captures the business of the Wear circa 1900 before its decline.

BELOW: A Dumbarton Road tenement similar to the one in which Alf spent much of his childhood.

ABOVE: The high pageant of the Clyde; the river crowded with ships in 1916, the year the Wight family moved to Glasgow.

INSET, LEFT: An aerial view of Yoker, Glasgow, circa 1915. Dumbarton Road can be seen stretching into the distance.

ABOVE & LEFT: Slum housing in the Gorbals (*above*) and Bridgeton (*left*) in the 1930s.

BELOW: George Green's Picturedrome cinema in Govan (now Ballater) Street, where Alf's father occasionally played the piano. Glasgow had the highest rates of cinema attendance in the world outside the US.

RIGHT: Boys' Brigade uniforms; Glasgow was the birthplace and bastion of the Christian youth organization.

BELOW: Glasgow Tramways female conductress or 'clippie'. The First World War brought many women into occupations previously the preserve of men.

BELOW RIGHT: Alf and Boys' Brigade friends.

ABOVE: Yoker Primary School on Dumbarton Road;
the building now houses a community centre.

BELOW: Alf Wight (third row, third from left) at
Yoker Primary aged 9; his lifelong friend Alex
Taylor is in the sailor suit in the same row.

The horse was the most valuable animal in both town and countryside, so worth spending money on when ill. And the horse was ubiquitous, the principal method of transport and locomotion in civilian and military life. Shetland ponies worked in coal pits, mules pulled barges, Clevelands pulled stagecoaches, Norfolks were between the traces of 'cabs', Highlands were under pack, thoroughbreds carried post boys, Dales ponies carried shepherds, Chapman ponies carried commercial representatives ('chapmen') – the horse was man's second best friend. Down on the farm, the increasing sophistication of agricultural machinery – epitomized by Jethro Tull's seed drill – saw the horse replace the ox because the horse was faster and did not require a tea break to chew the cud.

The other reason that the horse dominated the curriculum of veterinary colleges was snobbery. Working with horses was bad enough, but working with any other form of animal was beyond the pale.

When M. Charles Vial de Sainbel, a junior professor at Lyons, journeyed across the Channel with a plan for 'An Institution to Cultivate and teach Veterinary Medicine' in Britain, he made sure to locate it on high ground because marshy ground terrain 'exhales very unwholesome and putrid vapours'. This was in 1791 near St. Pancras Church, Camden, London. With due account for the translator's difficulty in translating Sainbel's rapid French – his command of English is best described as 'fractured' – there is no miscomprehending Sainbel's belief in the age-old explanation that evil 'humours' caused diseases. 'Animals are more frequently attacked by epizootic, endemic and contagious diseases than the human species,' he wrote, 'because we are protected from these casualties by our houses, clothing and manner of living.'

Sainbel was already something of a celebrity in England, having performed the post-mortem on Eclipse, the undefeated thoroughbred champion racehorse ('Eclipse first and the rest nowhere' as the era's racing pundits declaimed) in 1789. And so when M. Sainbel opened the door of the London Veterinary College, no fewer than 14 students signed up. The London Veterinary College offered a three-year course, after which successful students received a diploma describing the holder as 'qualified to practise the Veterinary Art' (no science yet). Subjects studied were: Anatomy, Physiology, Conformation and External Diseases in Year One; Surgery, Materia Medica and Medical Botany in Year Two; Pathology, Epizootic Diseases, Hospital Practice and Shoeing in Year Three. As a good disciple of M. Bourgelat, Sainbel made sure to put the horse at the top of the curriculum.

In an attempt to keep the riff-raff out of the profession, Sainbel laid down strict rules of behaviour. All resident pupils had to attend a place of worship; entry and exit were to be by the gate and not over the walls; and the porter was not to allow 'either drinking or gaming' by students in his lodge.

One of the sponsors of M. Sainbel's college was the far-thinking and influential Odiham Agricultural Society. They had a vested interest: diseases down on the farm were running rife in the eighteenth century. Something had to be done. Between 1711 and 1769, 10 million cattle in Europe had died of rinderpest. Unfortunately, the eighteenth-century veterinary profession was only interested in horses. A boost for the college – and the death knell for the old-style of farriery as horse-doctoring – came about in the year 1796, when the Committee of General Officers of the Army reported that, due to the heavy loss of horses caused by 'the total ignorance of those who have at present the medical care of them', it was of the opinion that the veterinary college afforded the 'greater improvement' in equine care.

To this end:

A person properly educated and having received a certificate from the medical committee of the Veterinary College shall be attached to each regiment having the name of Veterinary Surgeon, that the appointment is by warrant for not less than seven years, and that the Veterinary Surgeon shall have the same pay as a Quarter Master of Cavalry viz. 5s 6d per diem.

It was the first official use of the phrase 'veterinary surgeon' in Britain, and the first graduate of the London Veterinary School to be commissioned into the army as a veterinary surgeon was John Shipp. He joined the 11th Light Dragoons on 25 June 1796 – the date now recognized as the Foundation Day of what subsequently became the Royal Army Veterinary Corps (RAVC). Those who have served in the RAVC include a certain Brian Sinclair (the real-life model for 'Tristan Farnon' in James Herriot's books), a captain in the RAVC in the Second World War.

Little in the syllabus of the London school would have been of use to John Shipp, but especially not to his horse. In order to increase revenues, the London course was shortened to three months, so more students (and their fees) might pass through the mill, and it was determined that a tavern was a suitable location for exams for graduation – which were oral. On taking over the reins of the college, the new principal, Edward Coleman, issued 'Instructions for the use of Farriers attached to the British Cavalry and the Honourable Board of Ordnance', which included the following treatment for 'staggers', the erratic gait caused (usually) by low magnesium in the blood:

The horse should lose at least four quarts of blood, and repeated every four hours during the first twelve … The top of the head should be blistered (the hair being first cut close), one ounce and half of the laxative powder … should be given immediately, or even two ounces if the horse be large. The hair should be cut off from the hoof to the fetlock joints, and boiling water poured on the part; this should be repeated twice in the day. Clysters [enemas] of warm water and salt should be given every two hours (one pound of salt to five quarts of water). If the horse do not purge in thirty-six hours after the first powder has been given, repeat the dose, as before.

In addition, two rowels – leather patches with a central hole, pushed under the skin through an incision, to allow drainage of 'humours' – were to be placed under the horse's belly.

Inside, the first veterinary colleges were glorified forges. James Castley saw William Dick, the founder of the Edinburgh vet school, lecture in the 1830s, but the scene would pass for Glasgow veterinary college at its establishment in 1863:

One could wish to see Mr. Dick's lecture-room look some-what less like the appendage of a forge; but then he never has to lecture to 'empty benches'.

You may fancy to yourself a room of no very great dimensions in an old and apparently long untenanted house in Clyde Street. You enter it from the street door, and are immediately struck with the delightful confusion which seems to reign within.

Skeletons of all descriptions, 'from a child's shoe to a jack boot' – from a horse to an ape, not ranged in 'regular order all of a row', but standing higglety pigglety, their ranks having been broken by the professor's table, and their heads looking in all directions, as if thrown together by chance.

Over the professor's 'devoted head' is seen suspended a portion of inflated and injected intestine, with its mesenteric expansion dangling in the air, something like a lure for flies; whilst all around the room, and especially in the corners, are heaped together vast quantities of diseased bones, and other preparations, seemingly without order, and without arrangement.

Here we see no numbered specimens – no classification of morbid anatomy – no description book – all of which would tend to give the collection a pretty effect. Yet the lecturer has not only sufficient, but abundance for his purpose: his table is always covered with choice preparations.

That portion of the house which is set apart for the audience ... is fitted up with rough deal planks, set upon as rough props; the seats rising tier above tier, until your head touches the top of a very dark coloured ceiling.

Not long after Castley saw Dick in his veterinary school, the humble cow forced itself upon the reluctant attention of the horse-preoccupied veterinary profession. It took a disaster to do it. In 1839, an article appeared in *The Veterinarian* by Mr Hill, veterinary surgeon of Islington Green, warning of a disease attacking cows in London dairies. The clinical signs were 'inflammation and vesication' of the mouth and 'a continual catching up and shaking of one or other of the hind-legs'. People initially called the disease 'the vesicular epizootic' or 'malignant epidemic murrain', before settling on 'foot-and-mouth disease'. It ripped through the country, and a despairing Royal Agricultural Society of England agreed to subsidize a 'Pathological Chair of Cattle' at £200 per annum at the London school. The job advertisement required a person 'of some education – of more talent – of long experience in cattle practice, not past middle of life, and all his faculties unimpaired'. Twenty-nine-year-old James Beart Simonds, the first incumbent of the chair in Cattle Pathology, had all the attributes. He carried out a crucial transmission experiment. He wiped a handful of hay over the face of an infected animal, then fed the hay to a healthy cow – in which the disease appeared: ipso facto, the disease could be spread by contact between beasts. Simonds' experiment also showed that diseases in farmyard animals could be controlled by culling or movement restrictions, even if they could not be cured.

The calls on Simonds' expertise came thick and fast, but two cases, 20 years apart, were landmarks in veterinary history. In 1847, a sheep farmer in Datchet invited Simonds to view 'a peculiar eruptive disease' in his sheep. Simonds, on visiting the farm, diagnosed sheep pox, and traced the outbreak to Merinos imported from Saxony. At Simonds' behest, the government eventually passed an act of parliament in 1848 'to prevent the Introduction [to Britain] of contagious or infectious Disorders among Sheep, Cattle, horses and other animals'. And in 1865 a Mrs Nichols called Simonds to her dairy in Islington, London, where large numbers of cattle were dying. Simonds quickly diagnosed cattle plague, the first outbreak in Britain for nearly a century. From personal experience on the Continent, Simonds knew that treatment was useless, and again recommended, in the absence of a known cure, a 'stamping-out' policy, the restriction of movement and the cull of infected beasts. His drastic recommendations found no favour with the cattle trade or a government given to laissez faire. The veterinary profession was sent to sit in the corner. The Archbishop of Canterbury prayed for help from the Almighty: 'We acknowledge our transgressions, which worthily deserve thy chastisement ... stay, we pray Thee, this plague ... shield our homes from its ravages. Amen.' Only after 400,000 cattle had died did the country heed Simonds' advice, and in February 1866 the Cattle Plague Prevention Act was rushed through Parliament. Cases went from 18,000 a week to eight a week in nine months. The veterinary profession was the saviour of the nation.

Or, at least, no longer the nation's pariah. The vet's rise up the ladder in public favour was helped by a flood of Victorian-era inventions and discoveries that enabled the veterinarian to treat animals more effectively, from the stethoscope (1816) to the hypodermic syringe (1845) and Pasteur's confirmation of artificial immunity (1881).

The British had also begun their obsession with furry animals that is the head-shaking wonder of the world. Despite, or even because of, the fact more people lived in the city, a fascination with animals grew exponentially during the Victorian century. Visiting zoological gardens, bird-watching and butterfly-collecting all became popular pastimes. As did the keeping of pets. *The Veterinarian* published its first article on cat diseases in 1841. And so began the irresistible rise of the family pet to dominance of the twenty-first century vet's caseload.

An appreciation of the wonders of Nature went hand-in-glove with a dislike of cruelty to animals. Between 1800 and 1835, 11 bills against animal cruelty were introduced into the House of Commons, and set up in their wash were the Society for the Prevention of Cruelty to Animals in 1824 (later the RSPCA) and the Scottish Society for Prevention of Cruelty to Animals in 1839, both of which worked especially hard to improve the lot of horses, including installing drinking troughs and checking the condition of pit ponies. Horses, though, would still be worked to death: in Victorian Glasgow a horse pulling an omnibus could expect to work for just four years before being turned into cat or dog meat.

* * *

When Alf Wight graduated from Glasgow Veterinary College in 1939, he did so with a diploma that allowed him to be a Member of the Royal College of Veterinary Surgeons. The vet's governing body was founded in 1844; by the terms of its Charter and the 1881 Veterinary Surgeons Act, the title of 'veterinary surgeon' was limited to persons who possessed the membership diploma of the RCVS (and for a brief period in Scotland the Highland and Agricultural Society) and forbade anyone else to

> take or use any name, title, addition or description implying
> that he practises Veterinary Surgery or any branch thereof,
> without being liable to punishment; nor can such person
> recover payment for performing an operation, giving veteri-
> nary attendance or advice, or acting in any way as a
> Veterinary Surgeon or practitioner.

Every 'quack' who could stumble through the legalese of the Charter and Act rubbed his hands in glee. Horse-doctors, cow-leeches, castrators, and Uncle Tom Cobbly and all could continue in the animal-doctoring business – just as long as they did not style themselves 'veterinary surgeons'.

And so, when Alf Wight entered veterinary school in 1933, the quack was still going strong, and the veterinary surgeon had climbed up the pole of social respectability. He had not quite reached the dizzy heights of the human doctor, though; some clients still expected the vet to use the tradesman's entrance.

* * *

Alf's father did not want his bright boy to be a vet. Mr Wight suggested medical college instead. The social standing of the vet did not trouble him – other things did. Doctors were never out of work, never poor, never begging for work. One only had to step out through the door of 2172 Dumbarton Road to see that the veterinary profession could have no such comfortable certainties. The horse was the mainstay of the veterinary profession. And the horse was disappearing off the streets, to be replaced by the car. And in the countryside, the horse was being superceded by the tractor. In 1897 a Mr Locke-King bought one of the new fangled vehicles from the Hornsby firm, Lincolnshire – the first recorded sale of a tractor in Britain. The kingdom's farms would never be the same again.

The man who killed the horse was Nicholas Cugnot, a French inventor who, in 1769, built a three-wheeled vehicle with steam propulsion to bowl around the boulevards of Paris. Cugnot's *fardier a vapeur* carried four people at 4 mph. The age of independent transport with a mechanical, non-animal, power source had begun. Over a century of steam 'traction' engines followed in Cugnot's tracks, but they were mammoth-sized and tortoise-slow. Only with the development of an effective petrol-fuelled internal combustion engine by Belgian J. J. Étienne Lenoir in 1859 could relatively small and fast vehicles be made. Karl Benz received a patent for his car on 29 January 1886, and began the commercial production of vehicles after a trip in his car by his wife from Mannheim to Pforzheim proved that the horseless carriage was absolutely suitable for everyday use.

For two glorious centuries, the Shire, the Suffolk Punch and, in Scotland, the Clydesdale, had strode magnificently over the farming landscape of Britain, from valley to hill top. But if Cugnot killed the horse, the Kaiser and Henry Ford kicked it when it was dead and down. During the Great War, the German U-boat campaign, which targetted supply ships en route to Britain, brought the country close to starvation and it became a case of grow more food at home or die. The obvious answer was to bring more land into cultivation. However, since many of Britain's farm horses had been co-opted as war horses, tractors had to be imported from America to take their stead. To avoid putting British patriotic noses out of joint, US tractors were often rebranded for the Blighty market: the Parret tractor was rebranded as the Clydesdale. By 1918, Britain's wheat harvest was 50 per cent bigger than it had been in 1916.

The usefulness of the tractor to the land had been proved. Numerous small tractor companies were formed, such as the DL Company in Glasgow, which produced its 'Glasgow' tractor in a leased munitions factory. Car manufacturers such as Vickers and Austin also entered the tractor market. All struggled, however, to compete with the Model F and Model N tractors of Henry Ford of Dearborn, Michigan, the US of A. Although early models were expensive, Ford's assembly line methods of production brought tractors, as they had brought cars, within the financial reach of every farmer. Ford's Model T car cost a modest $440 in 1915, and his 'Fordson' Model F tractor was a bargain at $750 (about $14,300 in 2010 prices). Between 1917 and 1925, Fordson built 500,000 tractors at its Dearborn plant, taking 70 per cent of the US market. With stiffened competition from other US tractor manufacturers, Fordson moved production to Dagenham in England in 1933. Thereafter, blue and orange Fordsons became indelible sights in the British countryside of the 1930s. A Fordson in 1935 cost £150 for the basic model, £195 with low-pressure pneumatic tyres. The Fordson won a place in the heart of the farmer, congenitally keen on saving money. A US government test in the Thirties concluded that farmers spent $0.95 per acre ploughing with a Fordson, whereas feeding eight horses for a year and paying two drivers cost $1.46 per acre. Tractors, as the early advertisements gleefully pointed out, only 'ate' when hungry. A tractor put in the barn for night consumed nothing; a horse had its head in a nose bag or hay rack for hours. By 1939 there were 50,000 tractors on British farms.

The end of the horse was bewilderingly swift. In August 1911, The *Veterinary Record* reported that in London, a city in which there were over 300,000 horses, the London General Omnibus Company was 'selling off horses at the rate of 100 a week'. By the end of the month the company was expected to have withdrawn their last horse-omnibuses from service.

In 1914 there were 25 million horses in the UK; in 1940 there were 5 million, of which only 600,000 were on farms. Some breeds, such as the Norfolk Roadster, pride of nineteenth-century England, disappeared forever. The Clydesdale, which had only been developed by the Duke of Hamilton in the 1920s, went down to hundreds. There was hardship for those who lived by the horse.

In fact, down on the farm in Britain in the Thirties, there was hardship all round. A serious decline in agriculture from 1922 was hitting farmers' profits, while electrification and mechanization, both of which reduced labour costs, was making the labourer redundant. Whereas in 1926, 200 farms had electricity, in 1936, 6500 did. One pennyworth of electricity fed into a new fangled milking machine would milk 40 cows – a man's work for a day. And a man cost more than 1d a day to run, so the man had to go.

In the Thirties, unemployment rose in the countryside just as surely and bleakly as it did in the towns.

The British countryside in the Thirties was on the very eve of the 'agri-business' revolution. But in 1933, the farms of Britain – the farms on which Alf would start his student veterinary practice and observation – would have been eminently recognizable to John Constable, even Jethro Tull. Nearly three-quarters of the holdings in Britain were under 100 acres, they were run by one family, chickens scratched on a muddy yard, and barns were low and stone and supported by uprights that looked exactly like the tree trunks they were. The rural year was based on an ancient calendar of spring lambs, summer shearing, summer hay, late summer wheat and autumn calves. Cattle were generally 'in wintered' (put in barns) from October to May, to be fed hay or straw, or specially grown forage fodder such as mangels, swedes or kale. Since nearly every farm had a least one milch cow, the day was dictated by twice a day milking, at 5.30 am and 4.15 pm.

The major jobs on the farm were mass communal enterprises. When Welsh mountain farmer Thomas Firbank's flock of 1200 sheep required shearing, 40 men sat on benches, hand-shearing, sorting, carrying, putting on the owner's marking (with pitch), dabbing picric acid on the cuts on the sheep's body. The people helping were fellow farmers, their sons and daughters, villagers in want of a day's work. It was 'a social event of the greatest magnitude'. Firbank's wife provided the endless cups of sweet tea that kept the human shearing-machine lubricated. Any lambs still in need of de-bollocking might be done at the same time. 'The old method of castration was crude,' Firbank wrote. 'One man would sit on a bench, the lamb held between his knees, while his partner, using a sharp penknife, slit the bag and drew out the two testicles one at a time, severing the cords that held them.' Luckily for lambs, the bloodless Burdizzo castrator had just been invented.

Like most farmers Firbank liked to do his own animal-doctoring, and had a number of 'home-grown' cures, which included a treatment for intestinal worms in pigs:

A ground-up root called Snotin is effective when sprinkled in the food, but costs nearly a shilling a dose. So I used a mixture of castor-oil and 5 per cent oil of chenopodium. Great care has to be taken in the dosing, because the pig has a peculiar gullet. The foodpipe and the windpipe are very close together, and if in its excitement the pig takes the dose into the windpipe, instant suffocation follows. I once killed a six-score porker in a moment by careless dosing... However, as long as the pig can chew at something he seems to produce the correct oscillation of the gullet to swallow safely, so we thrust a thick stick in the same position as a horse's bit. In the middle of the stick was a hole through which we poured the worm dose.

Firbank's treatment for 'husk', a parasitic worm infestation of an animal's bronchioles and sometimes lungs, was linseed and turpentine, which was poured by the teaspoon into the infected beast's nostrils.

To the annoyance of the 'vi'tnry', home-grown cures and folk remedies sometimes worked, either by accident or design, a classic being Alf's own experience in *It Shouldn't Happen to a Vet*, when he is stumped by a reclining cow with a broken pelvis. The farmer, Mr Handshaw, happens to remember an 'old trick' of his dad's, which was to get a fresh-killed sheep skin from the butcher and put it on the cow's back. It probably acted like a giant poultice and annoyed the cow – so the cow got up.

Although there were more beasts-per-acre on the land than in the Middle Ages, the stocking rate was still 'extensive' rather than 'intensive'; a Scottish 140-acre dairy farm in the lowlands would have 28 Ayrshires, with 34 female stock coming on. The farm labour force would be, typically, the farmer, his wife, a ploughman, a cattleman, 'a lad' (a teenager on his first job), two male or female milkers, with the wife of either the ploughman or the cattleman acting as a reserve.

The most intensive farms were small dairy establishments on the edge of cities, such as Mr Stirling's in Scotstoun, next door to Yoker, which Alf visited many times in his college years due to the syllabus-demanding need to gain knowledge of bovines. Such farms carried more than one cow per acre, the beasts being fed 'concentrate' of imported feed (often linseed) mixed with millers' offals from nearby mills to produce a gallon of milk for every three and a half pounds fed. Demand was high and transport costs low, because they were situated next to a major urban area.

In Britain in 1933, it seemed almost everyone out in the country kept livestock. There were 6,770,000 cows, 17,986,000 sheep, 3,515,000 pigs and an extraordinary 56,426,000 chickens. The young wife with a few hens for eggs or the old man fattening a pig for bacon would be among the typical clients of the vet going around a rural practice in his reluctant, protesting car.

And if you had livestock, you lived in fear of disease. One farmer wrote in his diary in 1935: 'All our 4 cows passed TT [tuberculin] test – Maria-Dolly-Beauty-Carole. Vet – Mr de Garys from Reading.' Aside from listing his purchases of cattle (including 10 Ayrshire heifers from Mr Kirkwood for an eye-watering £192) and equipment, it was the only event he thought worthy of recording in his diary, save for major bust-ups in the House of Commons.

There were 13 'Notifiable Diseases', outbreaks of which needed to be notified to the police and local authority by the terms of the Diseases of Animals Acts, 1894–1922. These included cattle plague, foot-and-mouth, anthrax, bovine tuberculosis, rabies and swine fever. Sheep-dipping orders, formulated to control sheep scab, laid down that all sheep in England be dipped once in the summer, and in Scotland up to three times. In some scheduled areas, sheep had to be 'double dipped', that is dipped and then dipped again at a period not before 7 but not after 14 days. The process was overseen by the local policeman, who bicycled to the farm.

The owner of a sick animal had a number of options. Nature could be left to take its course, or one could administer any number of proprietary cures, all widely available, all widely advertised. *A Handy Book of Reference for Farmers in Scotland*, published in 1920, advertised 'Robertson's Terebene Balsam for Horses, Cattle and Sheep' as 'The Most Famous Veterinary Remedy in the World, Equally Efficient for Internal, External Use'. Meanwhile, a page in *The Country Gentlemen's Estate Book & Diary,* 1935, extolled 'Tippers Cow Relief, made at The Veterinary Chemical Works, Birmingham. SAVES THE UDDER – your source of income.' The Cataline Company of Bristol, in the same venerable publication, claimed that *its* drench 'For All Chill and Inflammatory Udder Trouble is Unsurpassed'. Six bottles of the medicine would treat 24 cows. It was also a balm for all farm animals, and could be dosed to sheep and pigs at one eighth of a bottle per head.

Margaret Leigh's experience of running an isolated farm in the Highlands, which she described in her famous book *Highland Homespun*, is typical of the small farmer's experience of treating sick animals. When Leigh's cow, Jessie, calved, Leigh could not wring a drop of milk from its 'obstinate and rubbery teats' for the bawling calf. So she sent for 'the wife of Rattray's shepherd, who had a great power with cattle'. She soon got Jessie donating milk, 'in little spurts, then in a steady flow'. When her horse, Dick, started rolling around with symptoms of colic, she sent for her friend, the Laird. 'He came at once, gave Dick a dose, and in two days the horse was back again at the plough.'

It was significant that Leigh did not call out any form of paid help. The rule of financial thumb was: the poorer the area, the poorer the farmer, the cheaper the animal, the less likelihood there was of calling out the 'veet'. A chicken on a three-acre croft in the Highlands of Scotland was never going to meet a member of the Royal College of Veterinary Surgeons unless that chicken was dressed, cooked and on a plate. A visit from a vet in the Thirties would cost upwards of 5 shillings, plus medicines. There were crofts in the Highlands of Scotland so poor that women went into the traces to pull the harrow because the family could not afford a horse or tractor.

The animal owner seeking 'professional' treatment for Fido, Dobbin or Daisy in the Thirties could try a 'quack', a veterinary chemist or the vet himself. A 'quack', the cheapest of the paid-for options, was an unlicensed, unregulated, and usually untrained practitioner of animal medicine. Unlike vets, quacks were allowed to advertise their services ('D. J. Jones Esq.' ran a typical one, 'All Dog Ailments Cured – Your Dog's Best Friend, Your Pocket's Best Friend'). The paper qualifications of quacks often gave them many impressive letters after their name – any quack worth his Epsom salt gave himself more letters than 'MRCVS' – but were never from an institution of any repute. Quacks were somewhat constrained by law, notably the Animals (Anaesthetic) Act of 1919, which required that the farmer 'must not allow a horse, dog, cat, or bovine belonging to him to undergo any of the following operations, unless the animal during the whole of the operation is under the influence of some general anaesthetic of sufficient power to prevent the animal feeling pain'. The list of operations covered nearly everything internal, together with amputations of the penis in animals above six months in age, and extraction of permanent molar teeth.

Some quacks sold their 'recipes' for the treatment of diseases, either to other quacks or direct to clients. One late nineteenth-century quack's recipes included:

The Hampshire recipe for to cure the foot rot in sheeps feet
Mixture for to make this Lotion

Get
A quarter of a Pound of ground alum and half a Pound of
sugar of lead and half a Pound of light Blue Vitrol

Notice
Mix this all right well up together in one Pint of water and
then apply itt [sic] to the sheeps feet with a feather and you
will find this to Be a splendid curative dressing for foot rot
in sheeps feet has [sic] this Lotion softens the hoof it does
not harden the hoof – always Be sure to keep this Lotion

airtight when it is not in use and also Be sure to have itt
right well mixed up together all the time when you are
applying itt to the sheeps feet this has Been used with the
very Best results.

Whether 'cows not holding the Bull' would be persuaded by the same alchemist's suggested aphrodisiac of 1 pint of warm vinegar, 4 ounces of cattle salts and an ounce of ground alum is debatable.

Some quacks' treatments were positively dangerous, and included ingredients such as arsenic. With proper dosage, arsenic can give a horse a glossy coat; of course, with improper and frequent dosage it can cause death.

Rarer than quacks were 'veterinary chemists' who tended to be chemists who doled out medicines for animals as a sideline. The veterinary chemists indispensable handbook was *Veterinary Counter Practice,* which, unwisely for veterinary chemists, could be bought by anybody for 2/6. This included savvy and educated farmers, who then promptly made up the required medicines from the instructions and tables therein, making the veterinary chemist redundant, and about to leave the scene as surely as the dinosaur. The vet was often the last port of call for the owner with a sick animal because the vet was the most expensive option. Called in as the last resort, the vet could not win. If the animal died, it was the vet's fault. If the animal lived, the farmer or the quack would claim that their already-given diagnosis and potion was the cure.

The year Alf started veterinary college, 1933, was little different from 1903 in terms of what vets did. Vets diagnosed illness, then treated the symptoms. If an animal had a fever, the vet treated the fever by reducing it. Very few *cures* for animal diseases existed. And the treatment consisted largely of 'posology', the making up of medicines.

A veterinary surgeon's dispensary would contain as many as 200 different chemicals, to be mixed precisely, the dosage dependent on the type of animal. To the fear and loathing of veterinary students, they were expected to know mixes and dosages off by heart for their professional examinations. When they qualified and were in practice, they could consult a posological table (see below).

V. Dogs

	PART
From ½ to 1 year	= 1
,, 3 ,, 6 months . . .	= ½
,, 1½ ,, 3 ,, . . .	= ¼
,, 20 ,, 45 days . . .	= ⅛
,, 10 ,, 20 ,, ...	= 1/16

Doses of the most generally used Drugs and Medicines for Animals

—	Horse	Pig	Dog
Acetanilidum	ʒi.–ii.	gr. v.–x.	gr. ii.–v.
Acet. Opii	℥i.–ii.	ʒi.–ii.	ʒ½–i.
Acid. Aceticum	℥i.–ii.	ʒi.–ii.	ʒ½.–i.
,, Acetylsalicyl	ʒii.–iii.	gr. xx.–XL.	gr. ii.–xv.
,, Benzoic.	ʒi.–iii.	gr. vii.–xx.	gr. iii.–x.
,, Boric.	ʒii.–vi.	gr. x.–xxx.	gr. v.–xv.
,, Carbolic.	gr. xv.–xxx.	gr. ii.–iii.	gr. i.–ii.
,, Hydrobrom. Dil.	ʒi.–iv.	mx.–xx.	mv.–x.
,, Hydrochlor. Dil.	ʒi.–iv.	mx.–xx.	mii.–x.
,, Hydrocyanic. Dil. B.P. 2%	mxx.–xxx.	miv.–xii.	mii.–v.
Scheele's, 4%	Half	these doses	
,, Lactic.	ʒi.–ii.	mv.–x.	mv.
,, Nitric. Dil. (1–5)	ʒi.–iii.	mvii.–xx.	miii.–x.
,, Nitro - Hydrochlor. Dil.	ʒi.–iii.	mvii.–xx.	miii.–x.
,, Phosphoric. Dil.	ʒi.–iii.	mvii.–xx.	miii.–x.
,, Salicylic.	ʒi.–iii.	gr. vii.–xx.	gr. iii.–x.
,, Sulphuric. Dil. (1–12)	ʒi.–iii.	mvii.–xx.	miii.–x.
,, Sulphuros.	ʒii.–vi.	mx.–xxx.	mv.–x.
,, Tannic.	ʒ½–1	gr. vi.–xv.	gr. ii.–v.
Aconiti Pulv.	gr. iii.–xv.	gr. ½–ii.	gr. ⅛
,, Tinct. (1–8)	ʒ½–1	miv.–xv.	mii.–v.
Adrenalin. Liq. (1–1,000)	ʒi.–iv.	mv.–xx.	mv.
Æther (Sulphuric)	℥i–ii.	ʒ½–iii.	mxv.–ʒii.
Æther. Nitros. Spiritus	℥½–iii.	ʒ½–iii.	ʒ½–ii.
Aloes	ʒiii.–viii.	ʒ1½–iv	ʒ½–1
	Quarter these	doses as stoma	chic and tonic
Aloinum	ʒiss.–ii.	gr. xx.–ʒi.	gr. ii.–x.
Alum.	ʒii.–℥i.	℈i.–ʒi.	gr. v.–xx.
Ammonii Benzoas	ʒi.–iii.	gr. vii.–xx.	gr. iii.–x.
,, Bromidum	ʒii.–vi.	gr. xv.–ʒi.	gr. v.–xv.
,, Carb.	ʒi.–iii.	gr. xx.–XL	gr. iii.–x.
Liq. Amm. Acet.	℥ii.–vi.	℥i.–ii	ʒii.–vi.
Spiritus Ammoniæ Aromat.	℥½–1½	ʒ½–1½	mxv.–xxx.
Spiritus Ammoniæ Fœtidus	℥½–1½	ʒ½–1½	mxv.–xxx.
Ammonii Chloridum	ʒii.–℥i.	ʒ½–ii.	—
Amylum Iodatum	℥½–ii.	ʒ½–ii.	gr. iii.–xxx.
Amyl Nitris (by inhalation).	℥i.–iii.	mvii.–xx.	miii.–xv.
	Half these	doses inter	nally
Anisi Oleum	mxx.–ʒi.	miii.–x.	mi.–iv.
,, Pulv.	℥½–i.	ʒi.–iv.	—
Anthemidis Flores	℥i.–iv.	ʒ½–i.	gr. v.–xv.
Antimon. Nig.	ʒi.–iii.	gr. vii.–xx.	gr. iii.–x.
,, Tart.	ʒ½–i.	gr. iv.–xvi.	gr. i.–iv.
,, (as vermifuge)	ʒi.–ii.	—	—
Antipyrin.	ʒi–iii.	gr. v.–xv.	gr. ii.–v.
Apomorphin. Hydrochlor.	gr. ¼–½	gr. 1/32–1/16	gr. 1/32–1/12
Arecæ Nucis Pulv.	℥½–1	ʒ½–ii.	gr. xv.–ʒii.
Arecolin. Hydrobrom. (hypoder.)	gr. ½–1½	gr. 1/10–¼	—
Argenti Nitras	gr. iv.–xii.	gr. ½–1½	gr. ¼–¾
	Half these	doses subcu	taneously
Arsenic. Alb.	gr. iii.–x.	gr. ½–¾	gr. 1/16–1/12
Liquor Arsenicalis (1–100) (Fowler's Solut.)	ʒii.–℥i.	ʒ½–ii.	mv.–xx.
Liq. Arsen. et Hydrarg. Iodid. (Donovan's Solut.)	ʒii.–℥i.	mxv.–XLV.	mii.–x.
Asafetidæ Gummi	ʒii.–vi.	gr. xv.–ʒi.	gr. v.–xx.
Atropinæ Sulphas	gr. i.–iii.	gr. 1/15–⅛	gr. 1/40–1/20
Barii Chloridum (oral)	ʒ½–iii.	gr. ii.–v.	gr. ½–i.
Barii Chlorid. (hypoderm.).	gr. iv.–xv.	—	—
Belladonnæ (Folia) Tinct. (1–20).	℥½–1½	mxv.–xxx.	mv.–xx.
Extract.	ʒ½–1½	gr. ii.–vi.	gr. ½–iii.
Benzoin. (*see* Tr. Benz. Co.)	—	—	—
Bismuthi Carbonas	ʒi.–iv.	℈i.–ʒi.	gr. iii.–xv.
,, Salicylas	ʒi.–iv.	℈i.–ʒi.	gr. iii.–xv.
,, Subnitras	ʒi.–iv.	℈i.–ʒi.	gr. iii.–xv.
Boracis Pulv.	ʒii.–vi.	gr. xv.–XLV.	gr. vii.–xx.
Buchu Infusum	℥ii.–iv.	ʒi.–℥i.	ʒ½–ii.
Caffeinæ Citrat.	ʒi–ii.	gr. x.–xv.	gr. v.
Cajuputi Oleum	ʒ½–ii.	mv.–xv.	mv.
Calcii Carb. Præcip.	℥i.–ii.	ʒi.–ii.	ʒ½–i.
,, Chloridum	ʒ1½–v.	gr. x.–XLV.	gr. v.–xx.
,, Hypophos.	ʒ½–i.	gr. iii.–xv.	gr. ii.–v.
,, Phosphas	ʒ1½–iii.	gr. x.–XLV.	gr. v.–xx.
,, Sulphidum	gr. x.–LX.	gr. ii.–v.	gr. ii.
Calcis Liquor	℥iv.–vi.	℥½–ii.	ʒi.–iv.
Calumbæ Radicis Pulv.	ʒii.–v.	gr. xv.–ʒi.	gr. vii.–xx.
,, Tinct. (1–8)	℥i.–ii.	ʒi.–ii.	ʒ½–1
Cambogia	ʒi.–ʒ½	gr. x.–xx.	gr. v.–x.

A vet in the Thirties was as much animal chemist as animal doctor. Vets weighed out powders, measured liquids, rolled pills, all from ingredients bought in bulk. Standby medicaments included liquid paraffin, castor oil, turpentine, aloes, common salt, iodine, soap-water enemas. Carbolic acid was the usual disinfectant.

On the top shelves in the dispensary, the heart of the surgery, would be 'Winchesters', large containers of raw material, brought by the drug salesman who came every three months. Poison bottles were always blue, bottles for castor oil usually brown. There were tea chests and demi johns at floor level, and in between, row upon row of brightly coloured liquids in glass bottles, red and blue, green and purple, with daunting Latin names written on them: *Potassi Acetas*, *Sodii Hydrophosphis*, *Hydrastani Hydrochlor*, *Amylum Iodatum* … Alf the student and Alf the young vet would spend a lot of time in the dispensary, with these 'noble names' and beautiful bottles looking down at him. It was an alchemist's exotic dream.

The label on the bottle had the name of the surgery and the instructions for administration, which were always picturesque:

'A wineglassful to be given in a pint of old ale, morning and night.'

'Mix thoroughly in a pint of gruel.'

'Dilute with a quart of spring water.'

'Two tablespoons to be added to a pint of water and given as a drench twice daily.'

Every practice also had its recipe book of tried and trusted treatments, which would be passed down through the owners. The

speciality of Nigel Carter's veterinary practice in Herefordshire was a concoction named after one of his predecessors, Barling's Mixture, a colic drench to treat diarrhoea *and* stoppage in horse and beast. 'It stops those that are going and starts those that have stopped.'

> *It was a mixture of aloes, turps, spirits, ether nit., etc etc and you gave it in a pint of warm water – or tried to give in a pint of warm water but you can try to drench a horse, but you're not necessarily going to get him to swallow it. And I used to get quite a lot of it on me and I would be smelling of aloes and turps for sometime afterwards. I can remember that in 1958 one of our assistants rang me up and he said was treating a horse for colic. He'd given it this injection and that injection, and said what else can I do? I said, 'Well have you tried Barling's?'*

He hadn't. He then did. And it worked.

Unfortunately, many vets' recipes were often no more effective than those of the quack's, and were given more in hope than expectation.

Near the dispensary in the veterinary surgery was a back cupboard containing the instruments of the job. Clippers, shears, castrators, fleams, probangs … Some of the tools were medievally grotesque and already on their way out in favour of the hypodermic syringe. Some of the most unlikely would linger on in a strange half-life; the probang, a four to five feet long bendy leather 'stick' with brass ends, was used to push stuck pieces of mangel-wurzel or turnip down a cow's throat down into its first stomach. (The leather stitching is perfect all the way along, so it does not scratch the cow's throat.)

Siegfried Farnon once used the century-old lancet-like fleam in the cupboard at Kirkgate to bleed a Gypsy pony with laminitis.

If the veterinary profession of the Thirties was still using fleams, rolling pills and making potions (or even dispensing the same red drench as the quack and the veterinary chemist), was the vet a practitioner of a 'black art'? After studying veterinary science at Glasgow College, Alf would indeed conclude that his chosen profession trailed 'the faint miasma of witchcraft'. He would be equally certain that he also learned art and science of the whitest hue.

PART TWO

PART TWO

THE WORST
VETERINARY
COLLEGE IN
THE WORLD

*'A momentous day! This morning, I started in the
Veterinary College. Crowd of new fellows waiting
outside; seasoned veterans swaggering in; stamping of
feet in lecture room; big thrill when I went into a room
full of dead animals; there's some queer fish here.
Those were my first impressions.'*

Alf Wight, diary, Tuesday 26 September 1933

The Glasgow Veterinary College was conceived in the city's
Sauchiehall Lane in 1862 when James McCall FRCVS started
giving formal classes in veterinary medicine for Edinburgh students
living locally. The student roll numbered ten. McCall had formerly
been Professor of Anatomy and Physiology at the Edinburgh
school, but had profoundly disagreed with William Dick on what
to do about the Rinderpest cattle plague sweeping lowland Scotland. Dick believed that Rinderpest could be treated, telling the

Cattle Plague Commissioners, 'I commence ... by the administration of mild purgatives, followed by stimulants, and after that, tonics ... where the disease has been a little more advanced ... a dose of oil ... lime water and tincture of opium.' He added that, with a change in the weather, the disease would disappear.

McCall, meanwhile, believed the only valid option was the destruction of infected cattle. To literally distance himself from Dick's views (which, as McCall divined, were fallacious), McCall moved to Glasgow where, in between acting as surgeon to the area's railway contractors, he was unable to resist founding his own veterinary school. Unlike Dick, McCall allied himself to the RCVS; McCall's school and 'The Dick' were ardent, and sometimes tetchy, rivals henceforth. No mean politician, McCall found friends in useful places, including Joseph Lister, who held the chair of surgery at Glasgow University and who reputedly conducted some of his early experiments in antiseptic surgery in McCall's premises.

In 1863, with a Royal Warrant in his hands, McCall moved the now formally established Glasgow Veterinary College to premises at 397 Parliamentary Road, off Buchanan Street. Here McCall lectured for three hours a day, sometimes by evening gaslight, and the facilities included a surgery, shoeing forge and rudimentary hospital. The first two vets received their qualifications in April 1865, with the examining body being the Highland and Agricultural Society.

With the job description of veterinary surgeon increasingly extended to include the duties of inspector of meat and milk, the demand for vets grew and the school thrived, with student numbers reaching over fifty. The college attracted a number of distinguished teachers, notably Professor George Armatage. Dissatisfied with the 'grovelling mediocrity' of the veterinary profession, Armatage was an early enthusiast of the longer training of students, together with rigorous examinations. He also believed that entry into the schools needed to be by proper selection procedures, telling the first veterinary congress in Britain, held in the Freemason's Tavern, London in May 1867, 'I hold it to be indispensable that the veterinary surgeon should always be *the gentleman* ... by education and training.' Within a decade, Armatage's desires had become realized, and the RCVS had organized preliminary and practical examinations for students, with the latter being done at McCall's own farm. It was a way of raising the profession clear of the quacks. (Armatage had another claim to veterinary fame, being the author of *The Thermometer as an Aid to Diagnosis in Veterinary Medicine*. Before the 1860s, veterinary surgeons diagnosed disease in the same way as farriers and quacks, by assessing an animal's eyes, skin and mouth. A cold, wet nose was good, a hot, dry nose was bad. The clinical thermometer inserted into an animal's rectum, Armatage suggested, was a more 'infallible test of approaching contagious disease, its gradual progress in intensity, or the more welcome approach of convalescence'. Armatage's other treatises included *The Sheep Doctor* and *The Horse: How to Feed Him, Avoid Disease, And Save Money*.)

In 1873, the college went on the move again, this time to 83 Buccleuch Street, a former water-pumping station in the Garnethill district. Following refurbishment, the new college opened its arched door on 28 October 1874.

Sixty years later when Alf Wight tipped up at Buccleuch Street, both the college and Garnethill were fading glories. In *The Art and the Science*, Alf's unpublished try-out for what would eventually become *If Only They Could Talk*, he recounted his feelings on first approaching number 83. He disguised himself as 'James Walsh' and wrote in the third person:

His first sight of the college had been a shock – a low, seedy building covered half-heartedly in peeling yellowish paint crouching apologetically among the grime-blackened, decaying tenement houses. In Victorian times the district had been the residential quarter of the prosperous city merchants and many of the houses had imposing frontages and pillared entrances but now it was a forgotten backwater, the haunt of broken down actors, purveyors of dubious trades, and pale, stooping women ... It was rumoured that the college had once been the stable for the horses which drew the first tram cars and there was no doubt that the outside appearance of the place lent weight to the theory.

Even the college's official history, *Records of 80 Years' Progress*, published in 1941, was obliged to admit that 'the college premises are far from inspiring'. But not, as generations of students discovered, uninterestingly located. In the tenement opposite the college was a brothel, where the endeavours of the prostitutes with their clients were eye-poppingly clear to students on the first and second floors. However, the college did provide its share of visual intrigues for the denizens of Garnethill. Animal bodies for necropsy were trundled along the streets to the college on the backs of carts and lorries, and overflow dissection classes were done in the entrance yard, in full view of passers-by. Since the college had the amenity of receiving the dead beasts from Glasgow Zoo for post-mortem and dissection, lions, zebras and an elephant all had their surreal hour on the stage of the yard.

The veterinary college at 83 Buccleuch Street was as unprepossessing inside as outside. 'There were no frills,' Alf recalled, 'no cool cloisters to pace in, no echoing picture-lined corridors, no lofty, panelled dining hall. There was a common room with a few rickety chairs and a battered grand piano which was used mainly as a card table and a hatch in the corner which served tea, meat pies and the heaviest apple tarts in Scotland. This was the social nerve centre of the whole building and all functions were held there.'

On the ground floor a single arch led into a quadrangle covered by a glass roof, around which were grouped the general office, a shoeing forge, library, staff room, the pharmacology lab with its bales of the sedative cannabis, Dr Whitehouse's anatomy department, male lavatories, a single female lavatory, the ladies common room, the ladies locker room, a board room and stables. Throughout the ground floor lingered the stench of formalin, used to preserve the beasts being dissected in Anatomy. Horses, cows and dogs were kept in open tanks of the chemical, to be hauled out by chains when needed for more dissection by students' scalpels. The first time Hugh Lasgarn, a young Welsh vet who attended a few years after Alf, entered the anatomy room at Glasgow, he was 'silently shocked':

I knew that, in order to discover how animals were built, they were best studied by taking them apart, piece by piece. After all, I'd done it with dogfish, frog and rabbit [at school]. But I wasn't prepared for the sight of large animal cadavers arranged in peculiar poses like plasticine models, grey, stodgy and in various stages of undress.

There were horses, skinned and lying on their backs, feet pointed rigidly to the ceiling; cows of indeterminable breed stripped of muscle so that the light shone through gaunt frames; from assorted tables sheep and pig heads gazed forlornly into space and, at the far end of the Hall was positioned a large preserving tank – when I cautiously peered over the rim I discovered it to be full of failed greyhounds. Above, ran great gantries with pulley chains to assist the

manipulation of the bodies, while fixed upon the walls were gaily coloured gazetteers of nerve pathways, blood vessel patterns and bone structures.

That ubiquitous, pungent aroma of formalin made Lasgarn's eyes smart and his stomach uneasy.

The common room, which would soon resound to Alf's piano playing, and where he would regularly lose money in card games, was on the first floor. The grand piano in question, made by Collard and Collard, was inventoried by the college's insurers as being in 'very bad order' and worth no more than £1. Still, the rosewood top made a terrific poker table. A 9' x 5' ping-pong table, pine benches, three photo portraits, a pine cupboard and a single coal stove with a stuffed moose head with antlers above completed the furnishing.

On the landing were two noticeboards and a telephone box. Off the landing were the students' canteen, the four rooms of the Chemistry department and the caretaker's store rooms. Clanging steel stairs led up to the top floor, which accommodated two lecture theatres, the examination room, a kitchen, two laboratories, and the departments of Pathology, Zoology, Parasitology, Physiology, Botany and Bacteriology. Conspicuously lacking from the facilities was a clinic. 'Lecture rooms were basic, some laboratories were sunless,' recalled Roddie Campbell, a student of the time. Floors were covered in worn brown linoleum or cork, and walls covered with cheap, dark vertical tongue-and-groove pine planking. Even in summer, the building was cold. Over everything lay an atmosphere of damp and decrepitude. The value of the frayed 180 books in the library came to a paltry £2/10s. Almost symbolically, the circular oak clock in the examinations room did not work. And eight metal rat traps were strategically placed round the floor.

Following incorporation in 1909, the Scottish Education Department had declared the Glasgow Veterinary College to be a central institution and allocated it £600 per year in funds. However, with the decreasing demand for vets in the 1920s, the government decided that Scotland did not require two veterinary colleges, and either Glasgow or the Royal College ('The Dick') in Edinburgh must close. In March 1925 the matter reached the floor of the House of Commons and after 'careful consideration', the decision was taken: The Dick was saved, Glasgow was to go. However, instead of accepting death by financial cut, the chairman of the governors of Glasgow College, Professor John Glaister, and the principal, A. W. Whitehouse, decided to carry on teaching. For funds, the college henceforth relied on local authority grants, donations and, especially, fees from students. The money did not stretch and on occasion the college's students had to ignominiously rattle charity tins on behalf of the impoverished institution at agricultural shows. One desperate college old boy, Alex Pottie, put a collection box in the waiting room of his Paisley surgery.

It wasn't only the building at 83 Buccleuch Street that was in need of renovation – so were the staff. As the college's official centenary magazine remarked, with masterly understatement, the cessation of the government grant meant, 'It was necessary to practice [sic] the strictest economy in the running of the college.' This meant that most of the teaching was done by part-timers with little or no teaching experience; at one point Professor Whitehouse was the only full-time professional teacher.

Some of these under-paid, part-time staff, Alf recalled

were old men snatched from retirement and forced to spend their declining years in an unequal struggle with boisterous youth. Others were veterinary surgeons in practice in the city who combined their daily work with lecturing and, in the process, imparted a practical and commonsense slant to their instruction which stood their pupils in good stead in later years. They, like the older men, had a detached, fatalistic attitude to their job and took the view that if the students paid their fees it was up to them whether they gathered knowledge or acted the fool.

Doctor Arthur W. Whitehouse, Principal and only full-time staff member, was a highly romantic American who had moseyed around the Far West in his long-gone youth, gold-digging and cowpoking. Somehow, he had also found time to earn an MA from Oxford, as well as veterinary degrees from British, American and Canadian universities. Before becoming Principal in 1922, Whitehouse had been Professor of Anatomy at the Fort Collins Veterinary College, Colorado. It was 'Old Doc' Whitehouse who interviewed the college's prospective students.

Aside from running the college and interviewing prospective students, Arthur Whitehouse put on his professor's mortar board to teach Anatomy. While Whitehouse's practical classes were enjoyable enough, his lectures were exercises in ennui. The Doc, Alf wrote, 'had a quiet, droning voice'. This was quite enough to send students nodding off per se, but to make matters certain Whitehouse's lectures consisted almost entirely in reading aloud from the late Septimus Sisson's *The Anatomy of the Domestic Animal*, which was replete with riveting lines such as:

> *The lumbo dorsal fascia (Fascia lumbo dorsalis) closely invests the muscles, but is easily stripped off the longissimus. It is attached medially to the supraspinous ligament and the spinous processes of the vertebrae; laterally, it divides into two layers. The superficial layer is practically the aponeurosis of the latissimus dorsi. The deep layer gives origin to the serratus anticus and posticus...*

And this was served up after lunch.

The lectures of Professor Hugh Begg, the moonlighting veterinary inspector for Lanarkshire, also consisted of word by word reading from a textbook, this time Monnig's *Parasitology*. Almost as venerable and genial as Doc Whitehouse, Begg was stone deaf, his hourly lectures not marked by sibillant snoring à la those of Whitehouse but decibel-rising riots. A notice instructing 'Hum while he's talking' was hung under his desk. And everyone did. Rubbers and pencils pelted around the room. Occasionally the loudness would penetrate his shrivelled ear drums, causing him to look up from his textbook, squint around through his spectacles at the dim figures on the benches before him, and exclaim, 'Wha' ... what's that noise.' If Begg was asked a question by a student, he'd reply, 'Ye'll find it in the book, son.' (His faith in H. O. Monnig's textbook – properly, *Veterinary Helminthology and Entomology: The Diseases of Domesticated Animals Caused by Helminth and Arthropod Parasites* – was well-placed. First published in 1934, it was still being issued in 2001.) Hugh Begg was doddery, but he was no fool, once retorting at his unruly students. 'Aye, ye aw think you're very clever but ah'll tell ye this, and I want ye tae listen carefully: ye'll never be a veterinary surgeon until every last one o'ye has strewn a forty-acre field wi' carcasses.'

In seeming contrast, bow tie-wearing Professor Andy McQueen eschewed reading from a textbook in favour of reading from his own notes. Unfortunately the notes, yellowing and fragile, had been composed decades before. With a glorious, serene detachment, McQueen stooped over his pages and mumbled away, not caring a jot whether the students arrayed in front of him listened or not. Like Begg's classes, McQueen's descended into riot, as Alf described in *The Art and the Science*, in which McQueen is given the pseudonym King:

The class took their cue from the considerable number of failed men left over from last year and stamped and cheered as though they were at a football match. This rowdiness always started right at the beginning of the lecture when the roll was being taken. When the name of Miss Debenham, the only female, was called there was an uproar of shouts and whistles while the poor girl who was naturally shy by nature, coloured deep red and sank lower in her seat.

The other outbursts came at the jokes. Professor King at the beginning of his teaching career in the later years of the 19th century had decided that his lectures would be racy and full of wit so he had pencilled in a comical allusion for each lecture. For nearly fifty years he had not changed a single word of his lecture notes so that successive generations of students knew exactly which joke was coming and where. For instance when he was discussing the snake Dasipeltis shedding its skin he would clear his throat, pause and say 'For Dasipeltis always returns the empties.' This was the signal for more stamping, wild yells and hysterical laughter from the class. The only time he ever looked up from his papers was at the end of his lecture when he invariably drew a large watch from his waistcoat pocket, gazed around the students with a smile of childlike sweetness and said 'I see by my gold watch and chain that it is time to stop.'

Pandemonium then broke out again.

Stuck on automatic, Professor Andy McQueen was unable to cope with any variations in routine or advancements in knowledge. 'Carmichael caused a laugh by asking old Andy a question,' Alf noted in May 1934. 'Andy of course was beat to the wide and started to hedge – with humorous results.'

Not *all* the lecturers were geriatric has-beens, though. Professor Andy Duncan, who taught Chemistry and Zoology, was a stern, authoritarian taskmaster. In the confidence of his diary, Alf called him 'Herr Duncan' and complained about his 'colossal cheek' in making them attend an extra lecture. When Duncan once let Alf and his fellow students leave a lecture early, they were 'startled' and 'couldn't think what was the matter' with him. Geordie Weir, who taught Alf Anatomy and Animal Management, had an inventive streak, and designed a horseshoe with a lug in it to prevent it getting stuck in the tram lines. For his services to the city of Glasgow, the Corporation named an avenue after him. Medicine and surgery, meanwhile, were in the capable hands of 'Professor' John Soutar – almost everyone who taught at Buccleuch Street ended up with that illustrious title – and his son Alexander, who were local working vets who could only devote an hour a day to teaching.

Then there was Professor J. W. Emslie. His hook nose and sallow complexion made Emslie look like a funeral director, which was appropriate because his subject was Pathology, taught in the fourth year of the course. Emslie left an indelible impression on Alf, a Brothers Grimm-like figure to inhabit nightmares for years afterwards. 'Pathology', Emslie boomed at his new students. 'From the Greek! Pathos – suffering! Logos – discourse!' But he was brilliant and absolutely passionate about his subject. Alf disguised Emslie in the *The Art and the Science* as Muldoon:

The name was like a knell – like the tolling of a great bell in an empty tower and the students heard its warning echoes from their first days...

Quentin Muldoon, Professor of Pathology, was a dedicated and in many ways brilliant scientist in the prime of life and though he may have questioned the justice of divine providence in selecting him to disclose the breathless secrets and supreme wonders of his subject to the shaggy creatures who shambled before him through the years, he did his duty as he saw it.

That duty was to teach Pathology and anything or anybody getting in the way of his teaching was mercilessly crushed. Pathos. Logos – the science of disease, the answer to all the questions, the brilliant light bursting suddenly on total darkness, the steady pointing finger of truth and hope. That was how Muldoon saw Pathology and made some of his students see it too. The others just learned the facts of it or he crucified them.

Walsh learned about him in whispers from the older students. He hadn't been at the college for a week before the mutterings started. 'Aye it's all very well just now, but wait till your fourth year. Wait till you get Muldoon.' When he asked these grizzled students to explain, they turned pale, looked at him from the corners of their eyes and sidled away. Indirectly he heard strange tales of healthy young men blighted in their youth and doomed to languish for years under the spell of the ogre. Over the first three years a picture was gradually built up of a pitiless, omniscient presence which had to be faced one day. 'Don't worry, he'll know all about you before you get into his class. Mark my words, every single thing you do, good or bad, from the day you enter this college, Muldoon knows. He's got you taped, laddie, right from the word go. Every mark in every exam in every subject. Every time you skipped out of the anatomy lab to go to the pictures. Every time you got drunk at the dances. It's all there in that big black head.' And the ancient mariner would shiver and look over his shoulder...

When the first three years went by and Walsh's class finally filed into the pathology classroom, the tension was almost unbearable. For a long time they had been romping into lectures, laughing and joking and the chatter hadn't abated when the lecturer came in, but this was different. The students took their place in comparative silence. There was an occasional nervous giggle but nothing more.

Muldoon was late and the minutes ticked by as the class sat looking up at the empty platform, the desk and blackboard, the rows of specimens in glass jars. Then the door at the back clicked. Nobody looked round but a slow, heavy tread was coming down the central aisle ... The feet, splayed *and flat, were put down unhurriedly at each step, and under one arm was a thick wad of notes.*

Muldoon mounted the platform and moved without haste to his desk where he began to lay out his notes methodically. He took a long time over this and still he hadn't even glanced up. When he had arranged his papers to his satisfaction he took some pencils from an inside pocket and laid them out too. Still looking down at the desk he straightened his tie, adjusted the handkerchief in his breast pocket then raised his head slowly and gazed at the class.

It was a broard, fleshy, pale-jowled face and the eyes, black and brilliant, swept the students with a mixture of hatred and disbelief. After a trial run the eyes started at the beginning and began to work their way slowly along the packed rows in an agonising silence. As the smouldering stare fell upon each member he seemed to shrink against the back of his seat and Walsh wouldn't have been surprised if his colleagues had begun to scream and fall senseless to the floor.

Muldoon, having finally finished his scrutiny, thrust his tongue into his cheek – a characteristic gesture with a God help us this is the end touch about it – sighed deeply and began to address the class.

He began suddenly with an abruptness which made some of his charges jump nervously by throwing out one

arm and shouting, 'You can put those away for a start!' The
students who had been fumbling with notebooks and pens
dropped them hurriedly and Muldoon spoke again. 'I'm not
going to lecture you today – I'm just going to talk to you.'

And he did talk, for over an hour in a menacing, husky
monotone. He told them what he expected them to do
during the coming year and what would happen to them if
they didn't do it. The time for the end of the lecture came
and went but nobody moved a muscle.

Afterwards Alf went down to the common room for a cup of tea, feeling as though 'somebody had drained a few pints of blood from him'. For the first time in his life, he had encountered 'an overwhelming personality'.

Alf would end up grateful to, as well as scared of, Emslie. In his early days as a practising vet, seeing animals with pneumonia, renal and cardiac conditions, the training Emslie had given him in pathology 'was like the lifting of a veil'.

* * *

When Alf joined the college on that September morning in 1933, 188 students were enrolled, including his intake of 50. No less than the staff, the students – 'rich, vital, outrageous and beguiling' – were a colourful host, and they were the perfect foil for the staff. Alf's first impression was that 'they didn't look like students at all;

RIGHT: Alf in his Hillhead
High School uniform.

BELOW: A typical
Hillhead street; leafy
with a terrace of
neo-Classical houses.

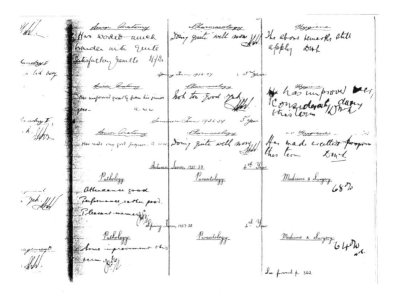

ABOVE: A page from Alf's report card at Glasgow Veterinary College. Pathology: 'Attendance good. Performance rather poor. Pleasant manners.'

OPPOSITE, ABOVE: The physiology laboratory at Glasgow Veterinary College, circa 1930. The Buccleuch Street building, a converted water-pumping station, was considered 'the worst academic facility' in Britain.

BELOW: Geordie Weir instructing students in the yard at Glasgow Veterinary College, Buccleuch Street, circa 1930.

OPPOSITE, BELOW: The pharmacy at Glasgow Veterinary College; much of a vet's life in the Thirties consisted of making up 'potions'.

ABOVE & BELOW: Students in the anatomy laboratory.
A horse is lying on its side at the rear; the equine
cadaver was crudely manipulated into position by
ropes attached to the overhead beams.

ABOVE: Staff and students of Glasgow Veterinary College, with the principal, 'Doc' Whitehouse, in the middle of the front row.

LEFT: Alf in his Glasgow Veterinary College football kit. Eddie Straiton, later to achieve fame as 'The TV Vet', is the dark-haired figure in the centre.

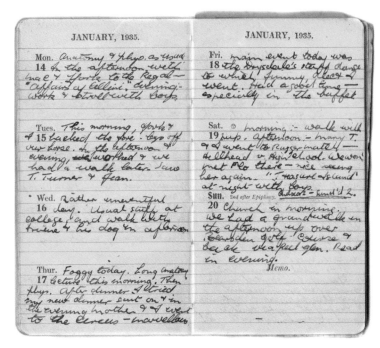

ABOVE: A page from Alf's teenage diary. He was ever busy. The 'pup' taken for a walk on Saturday morning is Don, Alf's red setter.

BELOW: Going up in the world; the Wight family moved to No. 724 Anniesland Road in Glasgow's Scotstounhill district in 1936.

PREFACE

This is a story of veterinary practice in
the Yorkshire Dales. The time is the nineteen thirties when the veterinary profession
and agriculture in general stood on the brink
of a scientific revolution which was to sweep
away many of the old ways and the old ideas.
Penicillin and the sulpha drugs were unknown
and over the vet's procedures there still hung
the faint miasma of witchcraft. The farms, not
yet overrun by the present day army of salesmen,
were relatively undiscovered and in the remote
corners of the Dales the vet was one of the few
visitors from the outside world. Country practice
was more primitive, rougher and harder than it
is today. But it was more fun.

                                    J.A.Wight

CHAPTER ONE

They didn't say anything about this in the books,
he thought, as the snow blew in through the gaping
doorway and settled on his naked back.

Walsh lay face down on the cobbled floor in a
pool of nameless muck, his arm deep inside the strain-
ing cow, his feet scrabbling for a toe hold between
the stones. He was stripped to the waist and the snow
mingled with the dirt and the dried blood on his body.
He could see nothing outside the circle of flickering
light thrown by the smoky oil lamp which the farmer
held over him.

No, there wasn't a word in the books about searching
for your ropes and instruments in the shadows; about
trying to keep clean in a half bucket of tepid water;
about the cobbles digging into your chest. Nor about
the slow numbing of the arms, the creeping paralysis
of the muscles as the fingers tried to work against
the cow's powerful expulsive efforts.

There was no mention anywhere of the gradual exhaust-
ion, the feeling of futility and the little far off
voice of panic.

He thought of that picture in the obstetrics book.
A cow standing in the middle of a gleaming floor while
a veterinary surgeon in a spotless parturition overall
inserted his arm to a polite distance. He was relaxed
and smiling, the farmer and his helpers were smiling,
even the cow was smiling. There was no dirt or blood
or sweat anywhere.

That man in the picture had just finished an excellent

ABOVE: The first pages of the
typescript of *The Art and the Science*,
later to be reworked by Alf into the
international best-seller *If Only They
Could Talk*.

BELOW: 'I'm safely installed in the wilds.'
The postcard Alf sent to his parents on
first arriving in Thirsk (Darrowby in the
Herriot books). He had been unable to
see 'much of Yorkshire for the rain'.

ABOVE: Alf in later life.
A successful author he did
not stop being the local
'vi'trny'.

LEFT: Mr J.A. Wight MRCVS
at the door of the surgery
at 23 Kirkgate, Thirsk.

at least he couldn't see any fresh faced young men with blazers and bright scarves round their necks. Later he found that many of them were countrymen, farmers' sons from the valleys of the Forth and Clyde and a large sprinkling from the Northern Highlands and it probably explained the tendency towards dun-coloured hairy tweeds and big, solid boots.'

And what did Alf Wight's fellow students see when they looked at him? Eddie Straiton, the fellow student who would become Alf's friend for more than fifty years, described him well:

James Herriot was a well-built athlete with fair curly hair, laughing eyes, good teeth and the tanned complexion of one who has spent most of his available time outdoors. Invariably dressed in a well-worn Harris tweed sports jacket and grey flannels, he could tan the hide of most of the lads at table tennis. He was also adept on the keyboard of the ancient out-of-tune piano stuck in the corner of our far from clean common room.

Alf's wardrobe extended to a plus four suit, bought 'under mother's persuasion'. 'I chose a rather alarming green check.' His 'signature tune' on the common room piano was Hoagy Carmichael's 'Stardust', which he played to roaring approval at freshers' night dances, followed by Cole Porter's 'Night and Day' and Duke Ellington's 'Mood Indigo'.

Alf made an early splash at Buccleuch Street by being elected to the Student Representatives Council, polling the highest number of votes in his year, 23, adding, 'I do not know how it happened at all' in his diary entry that night. The self-effacement was characteristic, but it was not difficult to see why he was chosen. He was too mischievous to be a goody goody, but had the solid values of his family, his church, his school, and was therefore dependable and decent. In photographs his face is always an open book. What you saw was what you got.

Like veterinary students the land o'er, Glasgow's contingent were a high-spirited lot, as the prize-giving ceremony, when the awards for achievement were handed out, demonstrated annually. In November 1933, the *Glasgow Evening Times* reported on the prize night's shenanigans:

A human skull descending suddenly on a cord from the ceiling to within a foot or so of his face was one of the shocks sustained today by the chairman at the prize-giving of the Glasgow Veterinary College, Buccleuch Street. The platform party was met by thunderous applause and banshee shrieks when they entered the hall in which the students were assembled. The opening remarks of the chairman, Mr Alexander Murdoch, were punctuated by loud interruptions and the speaker was threatened with early hoarseness. He was diffident, however, about having recourse to the water carafe because it looked suspiciously like an aquarium – a goldfish having been inserted there by 'person or persons unknown'. After his first half-dozen sentences, he raised his head and was confronted by a dark brown skull revolving slowly on a cord in front of his face. After a 'look round' at the platform party, the skull slowly rose to the ceiling again, from which it descended, 'spider fashion' at intervals, finally dropping with a loud bang on the table much to the alarm of the chairman. The students seemed to enjoy the command performance.

None more so than Alf Wight, who wrote enthusiastically in his diary: 'The prize-giving. What a rag! They hissed the unpopular profs, cheered the doctor, and sang "For he's a jolly good fellow", and bawled remarks at the big-wigs as they entered. I enjoyed it, I can tell you.' At the following year's prize-giving, the chairman, Lord Provost A. B. Swan, was greeted with the singing of 'Swannee River' and the descent on a string of a bottle of beer and tumbler from the heavens. Not to be outdone, the audience at the prize-giving in 1936 went for a pantomime theme, in which 'a horse' gave an impromptu performance, and a student dressed as a cat sat on the chairman's table. A 'Stop. Caution. Go' signal was used by the students to indicate when they had tired of the speaker.

Hi-jinx and high spirits were not confined to prize-giving. In the dissecting room of the veterinary colleges, pitched battles known as 'muscle fights', in which lumps of discarded meat were used as missiles, were common entertainments. Students with cricketing inclinations liked to bat the fascia, the membraneous covering of muscles, for six with a handy forelimb and scapula. Although strictly forbidden, 'muscle fights' went on clandestinely well into the 1930s. Sensible students put their pens and watches in the corner for the duration.

One of Alf's classmates, D. Byron Galloway, camouflaged in a blazer and plus-fours, was on a never-ending mission to bring anarchy to lectures of the elderly professors. He liked to fix an enormous nail file in a crack in the seating and pull it back so it 'vibrated with a startling boing-oing-oing-ning'. He peppered the elderly professors with paper pellets fired from a catapult. And if all else failed to unnerve the professors Begg, Whitehouse and McQueen, Galloway threw down an iron bar on the wooden floor.

Galloway got his comeuppance. Almost inevitably, doler out of his humiliation was Professor Emslie. One day, Alf wrote in *The Art and the Science*, where Galloway was pen-named as 'H. Crammond Dunblane', the class was *discussing the Clostridia and the professor was going at full pressure, rapping out questions, snarling and barking at the stumbling answers. Then, quite suddenly he relaxed and twisted his features into a rubbery smile. 'We now come to a rather abstruse point, gentlemen, so perhaps we had better consult one of our more advanced and enlightened students. Now who shall it be?' He darted glances here and there with a horrifying skittishness. 'Ah yes, of course, we have the very one here.'*

He pointed roguishly and, with a lilting, rising inflection 'Dunblane, perhaps you would be so kind as to tell us the sequence of events following upon the invasion of a tissue with Clostridium tetanus...

At this, Dunblane turned very red. Then the colour ebbed slowly from his face. Eventually he found a voice:

His lips trembled again and a hoarse croak came out. 'A gas is formed.'

Muldoon became very still. Nobody moved.

Then, terrifyingly, Muldoon threw up his arms and, eyes closed and mouth gaping, bellowed at the ceiling. 'A GAS IS FORMED! A GAS IS FORMED!' Then he rounded on the cowering Dunblane and sticking a trembling finger almost into his face, roared. 'Yes, thank you, you useless

> *clown, every time you open your mouth that is what*
> *happens – A GAS IS FORMED!'*

Not quite everyone was subdued by Emslie. A certain Brian Sinclair was moved to the Glasgow college from Edinburgh in the hope – of his brother Donald, at least – that it would buck up his performance. Instead, he got thrown out of Emslie's class for laughing, and had to go back to Edinburgh.

Some of the students at Buccleuch Street in Alf's time were near permanent fixtures. Since lack of money ruled the college, no-one got thrown out save for the non-payment of fees. George Pettigrew, who overlapped with Alf, spent ten years at Buccleuch Street but never got further than the second year of the syllabus. Almost all Pettigrew's time was spent in the common room playing poker on top of the grand piano; the only lecture Pettigrew attended regularly was Anatomy, out of respect for old Dr Whitehouse whom he revered. The affection was mutual, so that when George Pettigrew eventually left, either because it had dawned on him that he would never pass his exams or his parents' patience or purse had run dry, Doc Whitehouse was grief-stricken. Pettigrew became a vacuum cleaner salesman. Edward Gorman, in Alf's intake, spent ten years at the college, failing examination upon examination, until giving up in December 1943. Gerry Anderson served for 14 years, but did eventually qualify.

Farmers' sons, however, were some of the staple students in veterinary colleges in the first decades of the century. (Britain's most influential vet in the early twentieth century, John McFadyean, President of the Royal College of Veterinary Surgeons, was a farmer's son from Barrachan, near Wigtown in Galloway.) They were not regulars at the pool and card tables. Their times at college were of frugality and hard work. Looking at their names on the college register, Alf found it hard to read the names of their homes 'without smelling the heather and bog myrtle and hearing the screaming of the sea birds. Ullapool, Portree, Barra, Benbecula, Islay, Stornoway – they had all sent earnest, tweed-clad young men with nothing but health and ambition to see them through. They were scattered among the black tenements where they lodged usually with grim-faced women from the North who fed them on porage, sheep's head broth and salt herrings.'

Despite everything, they thrived: 'The only times the Highland boys looked really miserable was when they were enjoying themselves. At the college smokers [freshers' nights], they were inclined to sit together in a corner drinking impossible quantities of neat whiskey while one of their number paraded unsteadily up and down playing the bagpipes.' They ended these evenings green-faced, 'crooning their nasal gaelic songs'.

The Highlanders and the Islanders had no money to spare on such fripperies as clothes. In *The Art and the Science* Alf recounted being in the same Zoology dissecting group as soft-voiced 'Donald MacLeod' (actually George MacLeod):

> *Donald marched briskly in every morning wearing a shiny, celluloid collar with broad black stripes and after a bit it became obvious that this was probably the only collar Donald had – a sort of family heirloom which was handed down from his grandfather. Walsh used to pull his leg about it and say 'Well, now Tonald, that iss a peautiful collar you have on this…' and Donald would grin with delight and thump Walsh playfully on the chest. It became a pass-word between them but one morning one of the other members of the group made a crack about the collar and Donald, without hesitation or fuss, kicked him with all his force on the shin.*

The Highland contingent came from crofts, and were usually on bursaries from the Carnegie Trust for the Universities of Scotland. The Trust had been founded in 1901 by Andrew Carnegie, the loom-maker's son from Dunfermline who went to America in 1848 with his parents and made a vast fortune through grit, self-education, wise investments, and the ken to see that the future was made of steel. The richest man in the world, Carnegie possessed the soul of a Samaritan as well as the Midas touch. He was one of the first entrepreneurs to state that the rich have a moral duty to use their fortunes for the benefit of the community, the motif of his 1889 book *The Gospel of Wealth*.

Carnegie financed, among many other philanthropic projects, the building of 3000 public libraries across the world (660 in Britain) and the establishing in the bonnie land of his birth an educational trust, upon which he settled an endowment of $10 million. The Carnegie Trust for the Universities of Scotland was to use half the income from the endowment for the improvement and expansion of Scotland's institutions of higher learning, and the other half was to pay towards the fees of students of Scottish birth or Scottish extraction undertaking degrees at a Scottish university.

Like the Highland boys and every Scottish boy and girl going to university, Alf Wight had the minimum £18 a year grant from the Carnegie Trust; he also received a £10 grant from Glasgow Education Authority. The rest of the fees (which totalled £33/18s per annum), plus Alf's upkeep, had to be provided by his hard-working parents. Other students at Buccleuch Street had a tougher financial time still; for Eddie Straiton, all his parents could provide in the way of pocket money was 'tuppence ha'penny a day, five days a week'. Two and half pence was also the cost of a bus ticket to the college, nine miles from home. Most days he walked those nine miles to college in the morning, and nine miles back in the evening.

For those struggling to make ends meet, one of the perks of being a veterinary student was taking home the odd joint and cut from a post-mortem. There were also other less embarrassing student economies. Students shared textbooks which, even second-hand, were expensive. Eddie Straiton's book mate was 'Wee Harry' Donovan, whose staple diet, like many a Clydesider, was bread and dripping. Donovan used to supplement his grant by stepping into the ring as a flyweight in 'Premierland'. Alf's friend Pat O'Reilly gambled at the dog track (he eventually qualified nonetheless), while Andy Flynn played in an orchestra to top up the grant.

As with Straiton and Alf, the majority of Glasgow vet students were actually from Glasgow or its environs, not the wild exotic Highlands and Islands. Possibly as many as 75 per cent of the students came from within 25 miles of Glasgow's Central Station and lived at home. Still, rare birds did sometimes arrive on the train. Hugh Lasgarn came from a rural Welsh village and was perplexed by the Glasgow smog, 'green, evil and penetrating'. However, he found the Victorian architecture of the city centre and the university (which had moved out to Kelvingrove in the 1850s) inspiring and the people warm, and after five years could understand why Sir Harry Lauder could sing with such feeling 'I belong tae Glasgow'.

Rarer yet than Welshmen were students from Britain's overseas empire. Frederick Hempstead from Cape Town joined in Alf's year, as did the turban-wearing Qasuria Ashiq Mohd from North West Frontier Province, India, whose qualifications were a cut above everybody else's: he held a BA from Punjab University. Another Indian, BNS Chowdharry, was in the year above. Just one of the 50 students in Alf's intake was a woman. Margaret Cecilia Stevenson, always known as Stevie, had formerly been a pupil at Aberdeen High School. In the 1930s vetting was not regarded as a suitable job for a woman, and Britain's first woman vet, the legendary Aleen Cust, had been registered as a Member of the Royal College of Veterinary Surgeons a mere decade before.

Born in 1868, Aleen Cust was the daughter of the aristocratic Sir Leopold Cust, a gentleman usher to Queen Victoria. She enjoyed a free-range, horse-riding childhood in Tipperary, Ireland, and when asked what she wanted to be as an adult, 'a vet was my reply ever and always'.

Like Alf and a hundred thousand other vets, she took up the vet's scalpel and potion bottle because she was an inveterate animal lover. But plumping for a career as a vet showed a disregard for the gender conventions of Victorian Britain that dismayed her Society family. Luckily for Cust, she enjoyed a small inheritance from a relative that allowed her independence, and in William Williams FRCVS, she found a progressive veterinary professional prepared to champion her cause. Williams was the sometime principal of the 'Dick' Edinburgh college, but had since set up a rival establishment, the New Veterinary College, Edinburgh (which later moved to Liverpool University). It was Principal Williams of the New Veterinary College who, in 1895, accepted Cust as the country's first female veterinary student. At the New College, Cust did conspicuously, diligently well, first in nearly all her classes, despite initial barrages of jeering hostility from fellow students and staff. Cust was iron-plated against male joshing; she had spent her childhood with four brothers. Eventually, recalled a fellow student Major F. J. Taylor, Cust 'gained the great respect of everyone'.

Respect, but not acceptance. Despite a woman sitting on the throne of Empire, men ruled Victorian society absolutely. No woman had the vote, no woman sat in Parliament. And there were few bastions of male privilege more reactionary than the governing bodies of the professions, chief among them the Council of the RCVS. At a meeting of the Council of the RCVS on 14 April 1897, the chairman of the Examinations Committee reported that they had been asked to consider an application from Aleen Cust, 'she having produced the necessary education certificate for admission to the first professional examination', but the Committee did not consider they had the power to admit women to the profession. They were backed in this by the RCVS's solicitor. In his considered view, while there was no logical reason why women should not be admitted to the profession, the fact that no women *had* been admitted to the profession since the Veterinary Surgeon's Charter of 1844 meant that 'usage will now preclude her'. Once more, the doughty Professor William Williams took up his lance on Cust's behalf, pointing out that women had recently entered the medical profession and that the Council should be guided by this precedent. Again the Council voted against letting Cust join; again they sought legal advice. The advice of the RCVS's learned legal counsel, Morton W. Smith, was published in the *Veterinary Record* of 1 May 1897:

> *Although the word 'student' is applicable to both sexes, I am afraid the intention is manifest everywhere in the Act of qualifying only men. Having regard to this fact, and the fact in the case of the medical profession it was deemed necessary to pass a special Act, viz., 39 and 40 Vict., C.41 to enable women to become registered practitioners, I think the case is too doubtful to justify the Council to take the important step of admitting women without the authority of a court of law...*

In other words, Cust needed to take the RCVS to court to show why she should be admitted. This Cust tried to do in the Scottish courts, but the RCVS insisted the case was heard in London. At this Aleen Cust baulked – possibly she did not have the money – but probably she feared that a legal suit in London would embarrass her mother (her father now being dead), who had risen to being Woman of the Bed-Chamber to Queen Victoria. The ever-willing William Williams tried to ride to Aleen Cust's rescue by suing the RCVS for refusing to examine his candidate, but the RCVS succeeded in getting the action declared null and void by stating that they were not domiciled in Scotland, therefore could not be charged over an affair north of the border. This was a blatant lie; the RCVS had an office in Scotland, complete with notepaper bearing the address. An old guard on the Council of the RCVS was prepared to commit perjury in order to bar women from the profession.

If the Council of the RCVS hoped that the 'problem' of women vets had disappeared, they were to be severely disappointed. Aleen Cust decided that if she could not be an official veterinary surgeon, she would be an unofficial one. For three more years she studied at New College, departing in 1900 with a testimonial from Williams in her bag, certifying that she had attended the full course of studies and been found competent in all subjects. On Williams' recommendation she even obtained a post as assistant to William Byrne MRCVS, of Roscommon in Ireland, and so began a career in general practice.

In 1905 Cust was appointed Veterinary Inspector by the Galway County Council, with the task of administering the official orders and acts concerning animal diseases. As she was not on the Register of Veterinary Surgeons, the RCVS opposed the appointment and requested its overturning. Galway County Council maintained that they could find no other suitable candidate. The pages of the *Veterinary Record*, the independent *Veterinary News* and the monthly *Veterinary Journal* were soon aflame with arguments for and against Cust. To the annoyance of the RCVS Council, Galway County Council proved altogether slicker operatives, and neatly headed off any lawyerly challenge by simply titling

Cust 'Inspector', not 'Veterinary Inspector'. As 'Inspector' in Galway, Cust thrived. She also took over Byrne's practice upon his death, riding her Arab stallion to do visits or, if she needed a lot of equipment, taking her back-to-back gig.

Meanwhile, advertisements for 'The Cust Release Rope Hobbles' (her patented temporary shackles for a horse) appeared in the *Veterinary Record*, and she read papers at conferences, which were reported in the RCVS's own magazine. *De facto* Cust was a vet. Moreover, women were now being trained as vets in France, Australia, America and Russia, and there were increasing inquiries from the colleges in Britain as to why, exactly, women could not be admitted to veterinary courses. The RCVS Council was beginning to look ridiculous.

The Great War was simultaneously the saviour and the destroyer of the chauvinist die-hards on the RCVS Council. The vexed question of women was put into abeyance for the duration because the overwhelming concern of the profession was finding, maintaining and if necessary 'repairing' the hundreds of thousands of horses need for Britain's martial effort. On the other hand, the war brought women into public life as never before, with women taking on jobs previously a men-only preserve. (Cust herself drove off to France in her car to work for the YMCA, providing spiritual and material comforts for soldiers, before enlisting in Queen Mary's Army Auxiliary Corps, in which she worked as a veterinary assistant.) It was the 1914–1918 war, more than the campaigns of the suffragettes and the suffragists, which brought a revolution in women' rights in Britain: having been asked to do their bit against the Kaiser, women could hardly be asked to go back to the kitchen with no vote; neither could they be expected to accept legal barring from occupations they had so willingly, and ably, taken up in the nation's hours of peril.

All women over 30 were given the vote in 1918 and all women over 21 in 1928. On 23 December 1919, Parliament passed 'The Sex Disqualification (Removal) Act', which provided that a person shall not be disqualified by sex from 'assuming or carrying on any civil profession or vocation, or for admission to any incorporated Society (whether incorporated by Royal Charter or otherwise)'. At last, it was no longer allowable by law for the Council to bar women as veterinary students or practitioners. In October 1922 Aleen Cust applied to the RCVS Examinations Committee for permission to present herself for the final examination, Class D, under the four-year course. In light of Miss Cust's four years of training in Edinburgh and the testimonials she forwarded, the Examinations Committee judged that she only need to sit the oral examination. The *Veterinary Record* on 28 October, in an outbreak of generosity, welcomed the decision 'as a matter of plain justice' and wished Cust 'our best wishes for her final success'. Two months later the London examination results were published in the *Veterinary Record*, and in the results for the final year were the names of seven successful men. And Aleen Cust.

Cust's graduation was not followed by a flood of women seeking a veterinary diploma. By 1934 there were just 31 women on the Register. One prime reason for this low number was that Professor John McFadyean at the Royal Veterinary College and Dick in Edinburgh did their damndest to keep women students from enrolling, the very first step on the road to registration. Indeed the RCVS, although legally obliged to admit women as members, passed a motion in 1929 stating they were 'bound to disregard the sex of students who present themselves for the diploma of membership, but they feel they would be doing less than their duty if they did not make public their opinion that, in competition with men, women in the veterinary profession will always be under the most serious disadvantages'.

It was true that 90 per cent of vets were in general practice and 99 per cent of their work was with horses and farm animals, thus the work was hard and farmers were by and large conservative in sexual politics. Yet, as Glasgow's Professor Whitehouse informed the Council, some women at least could do all the usual work of veterinary surgeons absolutely competently. Doc Whitehouse and Glasgow were in the vanguard of the veterinary education of women. There may have only been one woman, Stevie, in Alf's year but overall the number of female students at Buccleuch Street was to rise steadily over the six years that Alf attended. In 1933, 12 of the 206 students were women; in 1936, 17 of the 284 students; by 1938, 30 of the 321 students were female. The college's special arrangements for the female intake were a loo, a locker room and a small ladies' common room. (The female students did not fuss about their appearance; there was little point, since they spent much of the day in brown lab coats patterned with blood.) A 'Women's Union' was founded to represent their interests. Towards the close of Alf's time at Buccleuch Street, the college even instigated an annual two-guinea prize for the woman with the highest qualifying marks in the diploma examination.

Alf's friend Stevie qualified in 1939, the same year as Alf himself. Of their year, 32 others eventually qualified as MRCVS. For all its high life and low facilities, Glasgow Veterinary College was extraordinarily efficient at making vets, as Alf's years of study there would show.

THE ART AND
THE SCIENCE

*'...found him fully qualified to practise the art
and science of veterinary medicine.'*

From the certificate of the Diploma for MRCVS

When Alf joined Glasgow Veterinary College in 1933, the length
of the MRCVS diploma had just been upped from four to five
years. His new life as veterinary student began with a year of
Chemistry, Botany and Animal Husbandry. He found Chemistry
with Professor Duncan almost as trying as Maths at school, a typical entry in his diary running: 'I found the Chemistry lecture very
confusing this morning – it's a blow not having had any science.'
His assimilation was hardly aided by the disruptive behaviour of
some of his fellow pupils; only a month into the term, Professor
Andy Duncan cancelled a morning Chemistry lecture due to misbe-
having students.

After the strict regime of Hillhead, the latitude of Buccleuch
Street was a surprise. There were lectures in the sloping theatres in
the morning, but the afternoons were generally free, due to the

shortage of staff. (Or as the college's official history glossed it, 'Glasgow graduates have the reputation of entering the profession better fitted and less 'Spoon-fed'... than most others. That is because in its studies practical knowledge is never submerged by theory.')

At Glasgow, it was sink or swim – it was the student's own choice. Even for a hard worker like Alf Wight, the easy-goingness of Buccleuch Street was 'wonderfully beguiling', although somewhat eye-opening for a boy brought up in a strait-laced home. After attending his first college 'smoker' (freshers' fair) in October he wrote, 'It was like the Curate's Egg – good in parts. The boxing was a new experience & very interesting – the light-weights were especially natty. I was a bit amazed at the character of the various songs & anecdotes which were rendered on the platform. There was a very good violinist doing his stuff. They are a queer crowd here – all types & kinds but decent enough.'

Within a week Alf was pounding the ping-pong table within a few weeks he was in a gang of 70 students having a raucous time at the Empire Theatre in St. George's Road, which ended with a student kicking the door. (The police were called, but rather than wait for the long arm of the law, Alf sensibly legged it.) He also, according to his own account in *James Herriot's Dog Stories*, drifted into playing poker round the grand piano in the common room with the old stagers. 'The only snag,' he wrote, 'was that I lost money. Not only that, but I ran into debt.' To pay back the money, he saved his tram fare by walking part of the way to College and lunching solely on the apple cake the canteen purveyed for 1d a wedge, which settled so heavily in the stomach it effectively ended appetite for the day.

His succumbing to the temptations of college life was typical, and familiar to generations of students before and since. There's a story told about Alf at this time, in which he asks a fellow student about an exam:

> 'What's the pass mark?'
>
> '40%'
>
> 'What did you get?'
>
> '41%'
>
> 'You've been working too hard!'

Yet Alf Wight was never likely to go completely off the rails. He was too conscious of his own desire to become a vet and the sacrifices of his parents for that. A bad result in a term test administered a corrective jolt: he got only 40 marks in 'Stables', when the pass mark was 45. The exam was not an important one, but 'I don't like failing', he wrote in his diary.

* * *

The veterinary syllabus had remained essentially unchanged since M. Claude Bourgelat set up the Lyons veterinary school in 1762. The most important animal to study at Glasgow in 1933 was still the horse, followed by the cow, then the sheep, the pig, and the dog, in that order. If Alf was disappointed by find that dog-doctoring was so low down the list, he was pleasantly surprised by how beguiling was the equus. After an introductory lecture by Weir on the points of the horse, Alf felt a 'thrill of fulfilment', as though he had 'undergone an initiation and become a member of an exclusive club'. He was, at last, in the veterinary fraternity. Or so he thought. As he famously recounted in *If Only They Could Talk*, when he left that lecture, he noticed a horse between the shafts of a coal cart, and he decided to give the beast the benefit of a professional examination. Stepping onto the road to give Dobbin a friendly pat on the neck:

> *Quick as a striking snake, the horse whipped downwards and seized my shoulder in his great strong teeth. He laid back his ears, rolled his eyes wickedly and hoisted me up, almost off my feet. I hung there helplessly, suspended like a lop-sided puppet.*

A crowd gathered to watch the free entertainment. Girls giggled. After what seemed like an eternity, the coalman emerged from a tenement block, and bellowingly ordered the horse to drop Alf, which the horse did, into the gutter, 'like an obedient dog dropping a bone'. Alf made his embarrassed escape, the coalman shouting after him, 'Keep your hands of my bloody horse. Dinna meddle wi' things ye ken nuthin' about.'

Horses let Alf Wight down in other ways too. Animal Husbandry included afternoon horse-riding lessons out at Motherwell (for which the college, naturally, charged extra), to which students went out by charabanc. After a pleasant afternoon buying breeches and a roll-neck sweater in the city centre ('I look really horsey'), Alf had his first riding lesson, which was 'great fun' and consisted of cantering around an enclosed bit of field. All the fresh air and exercise built up a formidable hunger, so afterwards the students all 'got some grub out of a wee shop' and stuffed their faces on the bus back, to the amusement of their fellow passengers. On 7 November Alf told his journal:

> *Well, I had my first experience of being thrown from a horse today. Paddy had not been out for a fortnight with the result that he was just too fresh & full of beans. We had jumping – I stuck on the first time, but the second time Paddy went clean off – bucking like a bronco & I described a beautiful curve in the air & landed on the back of my neck.*

This left his neck 'rather stiff' and his left arm and wrist sprained.

In his diary for Tuesday 5 December 1933, there is a single word: 'Concussed.'

He was brought home from Motherwell in a car, and the doctor prescribed bed rest. By all reports, Paddy had thrown Alf onto his 'dome'. Alf could not recall anything of Tuesday at all. Still, every cloud has a silver lining: doctor's orders meant missing the upcoming Chemistry exam.

When you fall off a horse, the maxim has it, get back in the saddle. A month after his de-horsing Alf was riding 'his fiery steed' again:

In the afternoon we went out on the old nags again – we had a wonderful ride and a tremendous [rag] in the bus. Stewart and Thomson did me up but I managed to leave my mark on both of them. I had the satisfaction also, of seeing Stewart leaving Dainty's back and describing a graceful semi-circle, finally ending up on a nice hard spot of road.

He would enjoy 'plenty of tip-top gallops' out at Motherwell, and almost warmed to riding, but he would never describe himself as a horsey person again. In practice in Darrowby, James Herriot always preferred to leave the nags to Siegfried Farnon.

At Buccleuch Street, the stables theatre was next-door to Anatomy, and for a dog-lover the sound-effects were not always pleasant: 'When I was at stables,' he wrote, 'they were cutting a couple of greyhounds' throats in the anatomy lab next door, and did they yell! I felt I wanted to charge in and sock the blighters who were doing it but that's just not done of course.' The greyhounds were rejects from the Shawfields racing track on the Rutherglen Road. Alf himself was getting his hands bloody because the first-year course at Glasgow included some dissections in the Zoology component of Biology, with the scalpel being wielded on such lesser creatures as pigeons and rabbits. The bunnies, Alf noted, were 'a trifle high but one gets used to it'. As for frogs, they were 'most unpleasant. Most of us sneaked out of the lab whilst old Andy's back was turned.'

As Alf's diary makes plain, he managed to squeeze in as much life at vet college as he had at school. Here is a week in the life of Alf Wight, first-year veterinary student:

Monday 19 February 1934

Stables and botany as per. Afterwards I had a few games of ping-pong and then walked down to Renfield St with Turner to get some cigarette coupons. While waiting for the bus to take me back I met Flo going into Skerrigs. However, she was with [unclear] with whom, I have been told, she is going steady so everything was very polite and formal. In the afternoon, not much doing and in the evening I wrote up some practical chemistry. Mother phoned late on to say all was O.K. in W[est] K[ilbride]. Had a walk with pup [Don] of course.

Tuesday 20 February:

I was rather fed up at Chemistry this morning and was glad when it was over. I had intended going to the Mitchell [Library] in the afternoon, but as I was leaving Hunter nailed me and said there was an SRC [Student Representative Council] meeting. So that filled in the afternoon. The SRC adjourned to Crounstonhill baths afterwards. In the evening I took Don out and wrote up some Chemistry.

Wednesday 21 February:

Geordie Weir had a horse in this morning and we had quite an interesting (and amusing) lecture. After that – Andy [McQueen]! In the afternoon, we beat Skerry's – not a bad game. In the evening I got down to it and got my Practical Chemistry up to date. Also had Don out. I am going to get into bed early as I was sleepy today. Adios!

Thursday 22 February:

Went to the Mitchell for a wee swot and then into Duncan's [lecture]. The poor man had a sore throat and could not give us a full lecture. Said he wouldn't be in tomorrow on the afternoon for practical chem. In the evening, feeling the pangs of conscience, I did the old work instead of boxing. Got to get down to it as the chem. exam comes off in 3 weeks.

Friday 23 February:

After lecture, MacIntyre and I had a game of ping-pong and then drifted down to the Mitchell and did a big swot till about 4 o'clock. It's a wonder we weren't given the order of the boot as I am afraid we were rather boisterous. In the evening, Jock and I improvised a ping-pong net and played till we were fed up.

Saturday 24 February:

Slept in this morning and felt rather seedy as a result. However, I trotted Don out and felt better. In the afternoon – the dancing class. I'm progressing fairly well and I think I could now swing a not ungainly shoe if called upon. Later I listened to Jim Catler [?] making his rugger debut for Scotland v Ireland in great style. Evening – Commodore 'College Humour' – very good. Walk later.

Sunday 25 February:

Delightful morning so Don and I got out in the wide open spaces at Bearsden for a few hours. In the afternoon and evening I 'plied my books' with commendable industry.

Alf acquitted himself with, if not glory, a decent showing in his first year. He passed the professional examinations in Chemistry and Biology (just, with 46 per cent, the pass mark being 45 per cent). Professor Duncan, his Chemistry teacher, wrote in his report: 'Is quite a fair average, not likely to be brilliant but I expect him to be steady.' As for Biology: 'I think this lad has the making of quite a good student.'

Things started to go awry in his second year, though. Sitting the professional examinations on 16 July 1935, he failed Physiology (with 36%) and Histology (25%), together with Animal Husbandry (37%). The clue to his decline is in his report from his Physiology teacher: 'Attendance Irregular.' Alf had been ill with a literal pain in the arse, a fistula, which, aside from its intrinsic discomfort, brought on bouts of sapping septicaemia. Over the years, the condition required several hospitalizations (including in 1937 and 1939, while he was still at college) and explains why 'steady' Alf would take a year longer than the set five to get his diploma. The same complaint also put paid to his progress as an RAF pilot in the Second World War.

Veterinary studies were unrelenting for students who wanted to qualify in the prescribed quintet of years. All veterinary students in Britain sat the same professional written exams, and the same examiner travelled around the country doing the orals. It was called the 'one portal system'. There was no lowering of the bar for Glasgow students just because their lecturers were generally below par. And the professional exams were intentionally demanding, usually comprising a three-hour written paper and one- to two-hour oral/practical per subject. So Alf attended his classes in the morning, then staggered with a pile of textbooks to the cavernous Mitchell Library on North Street in the afternoons, to write up notes and study. The copper-domed Mitchell Library was founded with a bequest from one of the last tobacco barons, Stephen Mitchell. Alf never did like the place. 'It has such a learned atmosphere; you can almost hear the brains throbbing.' And the textbooks he ported and pored over were all heavy in weight and heavy in content. There was Caulton Reekes' *Common Colics of the Horse*, Hobday's *Surgical Diseases of the Dog and Cats*, Monnig's *Veterinary Helminthology and Entomology*, Udall's *Practice of Veterinary Medicine*, Dollar's *Veterinary Surgery*, Hoare's *Veterinary Materia Medica Therapeutics*, Hutra's *Special Pathology and Therapeutics of the Diseases of Domestic Animals*, Miller and Robertson's *Practical Animal Husbandry* ... The Covent Garden publisher, Balliere, Tindall and Cox, who liked to dress their books with green hard covers, had the market pretty much sown up.

Alf's hours of study in the Mitchell with his Balliere, Tindall and Cox books was one clue to why Glasgow veterinary students did so well. Thrown back on their own resources, they developed independence and initiative. More, there is nothing like peer example to make a student succeed. Because some students toiled with their tomes, others followed suit. Underneath its 'play hard' skin, Glasgow Veterinary College had a 'work hard' body.

In the summer of 1936, Alf passed Physiology and Histology. For Animal Husbandry, however, he had once more, to borrow the euphemistic words he later put in Tristan Farnon's mouth in a similar happenstance – 'done alright'. That is, he had failed with 41 per cent. He was in good company; almost all his year flunked the exam at least twice, largely because of the sheer diversity of subjects candidates had to show mastery of in the hour-long oral and practical, including manipulation, ageing, harness fitting, shoeing, herd management, the principles of horsemanship, recognition of principal breeds of domestic animals, and conformation.

And so in December Alf Wight had to sit Animal Husbandry yet again.

This time, though, he had a helping hand. Sitting in on the oral examination was the assistant lecturer in the Husbandry department, Alex Thompson, who perched behind the funeral-voiced examiner, puffing away on his pipe. Thompson was new, young and very sympathetic to the students.

'How many orifices are there in the teat of a cow?' asked the examiner.

Candidate J. A. Wight pondered. Hesitated … then noticed a single finger sticking up beside the bowl of the pipe.

'One,' Alf replied.

'Correct. How many orifices in the teat of a mare?'

Out of the nicotine miasma emerged two pale digits.

'Two,' answered Alf nonchalantly…

* * *

By the time Alf passed Animal Husbandry at Christmas 1936, the Wight family had moved from 2172 Dumbarton Road, Yoker, to 724 Anniesland Road, Scotstounhill. It was a mile eastwards in distance, a continent away in atmosphere. Anniesland Road was leafy, quiet and distinctly middle class, and Hannah must have felt, as she entered her new rented semi-detached house with its front lawn, that she had arrived at her right place in life. The previous tenant had been a dentist. Her near neighbours were doctors, and the Scotstounhill Bowling and Tennis Club was a step along the road at number 633.

At Anniesland Road, Hannah was able to spread out her dressmaking business, Alf had an upstairs bedroom with views – of the Kilpatrick Hills and the Campsie Fells – and Jim was nearer the fish and chip shop on Dumbarton Road of which he was the proprietor and which was now his main source of income. But that was the thing about Alf's parents; they were always trying something to make money. 'Ye olde shoppe,' Alf called his father's emporium, and sometimes lent a hand in the evenings and weekends. A few years later Pop Wight found Anniesland equally convenient for a job as a shipyard clerk at Yarrow's.

Aside from the money gathered from their own efforts, Jim and Hannah could afford the rental on 724 Anniesland Road because Jim's father had died, leaving a tidy fortune of £7,366. Like his son with his music, Jim senior had long had another interest beyond the shipyard. His was property speculation, and when he died he owned no less than six houses in Sunderland, to be shared among his children. At this stage of the Thirties, two-thirds of the British deceased left an estate of less than £100.

The Yoker the Wights had left behind was not the Yoker they had arrived in in 1916. It had become a world of quiet because shipbuilding had all but stopped on the Clyde; in the famous phrase from George Blake's 1935 novel *The Shipbuilders*, the river had become a 'high, tragic pageant' of yards with empty berths, and weeds growing among the keel blocks and cranes. Nor had Yoker escaped the deprivations of the Depression in all their existential misery and violence, as one dramatic entry in Alf's diary shows: 'Mr Ballantyne cut Mrs Ballantyne's throat tonight – she's dead and he's been taken away – It's terrible for Bunt and Jack.' The Ballantynes lived around the corner from the Wights. Less than a minute away. The murder made the nation's paper of record, *The Scotsman*:

Following the discovery on Monday evening of a middle-aged woman lying fatally injured in a tenement house in the Yoker district of Glasgow, her husband appeared at Glasgow Marine Police Court yesterday, and was formally remanded in custody for two days.

The man, John Ballantyne (57), was charged with having on May 7, in a house at 10 Lady Anne Street, assaulted Christina Olsen or Ballantyne, his wife, residing there, cut her on the throat with a razor or other sharp instrument and murdered her.

A grey-haired man of slim build, and neatly dressed in a blue suit, Ballantyne presented a dejected appearance during the brief court proceedings before Bailie Alexander McLean. While the charge was being read out he bowed his

head on his arms, which were resting on the rails of the
dock. His right hand was heavily bandaged.

SCREAMS ALARM NEIGHBOURS

About nine o'clock on Monday night screams and the sound
of a struggle were heard in the Ballantynes' house, and
neighbours informed the police. When entrance was effected
the woman was found lying in the kitchen in a pool of
blood. She was rushed by ambulance to the Western Infir-
mary but died on the way to the institution. Ballantyne was
arrested in the house of a neighbour.

A coppersmith to trade, Ballantyne had been employed
on the Cunarder at Clydebank, but had been paid off when
work on the vessel was stopped. He found employment in
another yard, but again had lost his position.

For the Wights the move to Scotstounhill was an escape from a
Yoker on the slide.

There was something else about Scotstounhill apart from its
social respectability; with its trees and relatively low-density housing it was an altogether healthier environment, and both Hannah
and Pop had suffered illnesses beyond the usual sniffles and aches
of middle age. His mother's health, in particular, worried Alf. When
she was ill, he was sad. Conversely, he told his diary: 'There's

Mother laughing just now. It is the world's greatest tonic to me when I know she is happy.'

* * *

From his new home at Scotstounhill, Alf Wight returned to College in September 1936 in good health and mind. His marks soared. Doc Whitehouse, teaching Alf Anatomy, wrote happily, 'Has improved greatly from his junior year. Very good progress.'

Other students were not doing so well. Every term someone toppled by the wayside, to have the words 'LEFT COLLEGE' inked under their names in the college register. By the autumn term of 1936, nine of Alf's year had quit, among them two of the Islanders, Norman Mackay and Bantyne Maclean, who both had attended Portree Secondary School on Skye. Homesickness possibly claimed them, or the need to be down on the family farm, since neither had been doing that badly. Alf was not going to join the fallen, despite the upcoming *Materia Medica* (Pharmacology), universally regarded as being one of the Beecher's Brooks of the diploma course. As Alf recalled years later, passing 'the vast and complicated subject of Materia Medica' consisted of learning an 'endless list of medicaments' with Latin names, and actions on the differing types of animal. Doctors of humans 'have only to learn one dosage rate for their patients, but a vet has to know five.' That is, for the holy quintet of the horse, ox, sheep, pig and dog. Alf's friend Eddie Straiton likewise considered *Materia Medica* a dreadful subject to study, 'full of intricate facts about size and shape of drug crystals, odours and so on,' and found it well nigh impossible to retain the details in his mind for any length of time. With the professional exams approaching and a whole book to learn, Straiton suffered nightly panics at what he had forgotten and what he had yet to learn. 'Eventually time ran out', he wrote, 'and I went to sleep at ten o'clock the night before the exam, resigned to my fate. At four in the morning I woke with a start. My mind was crystal clear and a voice kept drumming in my ears, "Do morphine! Do strychnine! Do morphine! Do strychnine!" There and then I opened the text-book and read through the chapters on morphine and strychnine again and again.' When he sat down in the Maclay Hall that morning and turned over his paper, he stared in wonder. All four of the compulsory questions were on morphine and strychnine. 'The Good Lord had guided my mind,' he concluded. 'How else could this be explained?'

Few students were wholly unmoved by the unseen and mesmerizing natural worlds opened up to them, whether by taking the layers of skin off an animal in Senior Anatomy or by looking down a microscope in Histology. Whilst endlessly interesting to the brain, though, Senior Anatomy also required a stomach as strong as the galvanized bins in the lab into which used animal bits were dumped. Some novice always swiftly exited the carcase strewn lab, where the 41 hanging light bulbs threw expressionist shadows on to the walls, when their scalpel first entered the flesh of a dog.

Strapped to metal-topped tables, dogs were dissected by two students so they could talk and discuss what they found (or should have found), while up to four students would work on a horse, which was made accessible despite its size by crude feats of engineering, involving ropes from a gantry.

Worse than flexing a scalpel was the dismembering of an animal; when the college insurers performed their audit, they listed among the Anatomy lab's equipment: 1 large and 1 small pair of pruning shears, 3 saws, 7 butcher's knives, 2 hammers, 1 set of pincers, 7 cold chisels and a fret saw. Veterinary Hygiene, which with Senior Anatomy and Pharmacology, comprised the triumvirate of Third Year subjects, was also a test for the faint-stomached because it involved visits to Glasgow's meat market with its hundreds of hooked-up animal cadavers.

* * *

College hops were so popular at Glasgow that there was barely room to swing a cat, let alone a human partner to a jazz number. To ensure, however, he did not display 'an ungainly shoe if called upon', Alf had taken dancing lessons.

Dance nights followed a set pattern, which involved several rounds of beer with whiskey chasers at a nearby pub, maybe even one of the newly opened art deco pubs, with their chrome-edged bar-tops and peach mirrors. These bars welcomed women – when accompanied by men – and served fashionable cocktails such as

Manhattan and Angel's Kiss. (But better an Angel's Kiss than a Glasgow Kiss.)

Alf left an immortal picture in words of 'dance night' at college in the unpublished novel *The Art and the Science*, in which he is once again 'Walsh'. The evening commenced with some avant-dance drinking at Danny Neal's bar, from which the boisterous veterinary students were then unceremoniously evicted:

Outside, the rain was falling in a steady downpour and Walsh found it hard to focus on the lights of the trams as they swished through the wet streets. The students straggled along the pavement in an unsteady crocodile with Aly Gordon in front holding up a life-size, cardboard Johnny Walker figure which he had removed on his way out of the pub. The busy city square was alive with traffic but Aly headed confidently into the midst of it with the others following blindly. Brakes squealed, tram bells clanged, drivers yelled but the strange procession staggered on.

Walsh was at the back, holding Bernie firmly by his coat collar. It was the only way Bernie could stand up. His mouth hung open, his eyes were shut and he put one foot in front of the other like a robot.

They reached New Town Road on the other side of the square and started the long climb up Montrose Street. It was an ill-lit, seedy street and the rain streamed down the

crumbling frontages of the houses into the gloomy base-
ments beneath. Near the top was the college.

Bernie's condition deteriorated rapidly on the way up
and he had to make frequent stops to press his face against
the wet iron railings till Walsh dragged him on again. This
way they fell behind and only caught up when the main
party halted under a street lamp. There had been a sugges-
tion that they should save the price of admission by crashing
past the officials at the entrance and the idea spread like a
fire in dry grass.

There was a lot of shouting and arm waving. A general
elation at the prospect of a little violence.

Fifty yards away, light streamed out through the college
arch on to the pavements, and beyond, in the covered yard,
there were signs of activity. Tables were being dragged
across to form a barricade while the members of the dance
committee kept an anxious watch. Soon there was an
unbroken line of tables and behind, Walsh could recognise
most of the rugby fifteen standing shoulder to shoulder,
quietly waiting. They looked businesslike and disciplined in
contrast with the mob outside.

Walsh got both hands on Bernie's collar and shook him.
'Look, Bernie we're going to make a dash for it through the
arch. Can you run?'

Bernie stared blearily at the entrance. 'Run? Sure I can run. Run like hell. Faster than anybody.' He looked sleepy but aggressive. Suddenly he bawled out 'Come, on, let's get in there!' and started forward at an unsteady gallop.

Walsh grabbed his collar again. 'No, no, you've got to keep to the middle of the bunch. Keep to the middle and you'll be all right. They want the biggest in front – that means Ally and me – so I've got to leave you.'

There was a final consultation under the street lamp then the charge commenced. Aly Gordon was an inspiring figure pounding along in front, his Johnny Walker sign held high and a Highland war cry bubbling from his lips. Behind him the motley band puffed and reeled.

The big guards in the archway set themselves. Aly's fifteen stones hit the tables and he went down with two committee men on top of him. Walsh jumped over the struggling bodies, one or two fists thumped him, but he was through the breach and running hard across the yard. He heard sounds of strife behind him but didn't tarry. A minute later he was upstairs hanging his coat in the cloakroom and looking innocent.

He washed his hands and face, combed his hair and strolled downstairs into the yard. The battle had been brief and the combatants had dispersed except for a few wounded who were sitting propped against a wall and receiving first aid.

Tables and chairs were scattered around and a group of students were gathered round a still figure stretched on the concrete. Walsh quickened his steps – the figure had spectacles. It was Bernie all right, flat on his back, eyes closed and a red bruise on the side of his face.

'What happened?' Walsh said, shame flooding through him.

A large man turned towards him – Ian Clelland, the college's number one rugby player, a second row forward on the international fringe. Off the field he was a gentle, slow-speaking character. He grinned apologetically. 'Young Hill, here, came lolloping in at the rear of the raiding party and I grabbed him. I only wanted to get his entrance money but he belted me one in the eye. I was so bloody surprised that I tapped him on the jaw. I didn't mean to hurt him.' He scratched his head and looked down anxiously at the inert form.

Walsh knelt down and raised Bernie's head. 'He's been here nearly five years and finally he comes to a dance. And now look at him – he isn't going to see much of it, poor little beggar. Anyway, we can't leave him lying here.'

He looked round the yard and saw several long wooden boxes filled with shavings. They were about seven feet long and had carried a supply of new microscopes and other laboratory equipment.

'The very thing,' Walsh said. 'We can put him in one of those and I can keep an eye on him from the common room window. Come on, Ian, let's get him over there.'

They carried Bernie's frail body easily over to the first box. But there was a snag. Don Noyce was already there, deeply embedded in the shavings. He was still wearing his flat cap and his face had a ghastly bluish tinge.

Clelland peered down at the pinched nose and the motionless, sunken eyelids. 'He's not dead, is he?'

'Not him. He always goes that colour. Let's try this other one.'

This, too, was occupied. Peter Napier was comfortably in residence, a peaceful half smile on his sleeping face.

'Good God, he's done it again,' Walsh cried. 'But how about his girlfriend?'

'Over there, by the door,' Clelland hissed between his teeth.

Walsh looked up and saw a girl with shining fair hair and a cross expression, her hands thrust deep into the pockets of a tweed coat. Hugh Mills was talking persuasively to her but didn't seem to be making any headway. She was staring in disbelief at the unheeding face of her escort protruding from the shavings.

But Bernie was beginning to get heavy and they bore him over to the third box. It was empty and they made him comfortable in it. Walsh was relieved to see that Bernie was coming round. He stirred, smiled at them and went to sleep again. The box was ideally situated directly under the windows of the common room where the dance was being held.

Walsh went across the yard, through the door and up the flight of stone steps. Ahead of him he could hear the muffled thud thud of the drums and the thin sound of a muted trumpet. He pushed open the swing doors at the top and stepped inside into the noise and heat.

He found he had to lean against a wall. In his concern over Bernie he had forgotten about the long succession of whiskies and beer he had drunk himself. The dance floor swayed and surged up at him. He put the palms of his hands against the wall behind him and closed his eyes. But this was worse. Everything stopped swaying and joined in a mad whirl. He opened his eyes quickly, edged his way along the wall and slid into a chair to think things out.

He was dimly aware of couples dancing past him and over to the left at the far end of the hall he could hear the band. He was, as yet, unable to see it. It was beyond his range. He decided to concentrate and found that, by closing one eye and staring fixedly with the other, the band would swim into focus for a few seconds at a time. He used this technique to explore the place, working his way with his one *eye slowly along the walls. When he reached the spot dead opposite he realised that somebody was smiling over at him.*

He recognised Drew Turner, one of the more respectable students. Drew hadn't been with the drinking party at Danny Neal's and had his steady girl with him. She wore her dark hair in a bun and had a sweet, innocent Sunday school face. Walsh gathered from Drew's waves and the girl's encouraging smiles that he was expected to go over and be introduced, but he didn't feel up to attempting the journey across the floor.

After a bit, the couple came over. Walsh got up carefully and the introductions were made. They sat down with the girl between them and it was clear there was no escape. He would cause mortal offence if he didn't ask her to dance. He took a deep breath and turned towards her.

'Would you care to dance?' he muttered.

'Thank you, I'd love to,' the girl said brightly, jumping up and smoothing down her dress.

Groaning inwardly, Walsh got slowly to his feet, clasped her and set out across the floor. He didn't feel himself fall – he just changed his position effortlessly so that he was lying flat on the boards with the girl on top of him, her startled face pressed against his own.

Then he saw Drew. He was helping them up with a strained smile. They set off again and this time Walsh felt he was doing better. He actually gained enough confidence to attempt a twiddly bit and it was with genuine surprise that he realised they were once more on the floor, the girl underneath this time.

Drew was immediately with them again but he wasn't smiling. He helped his girl up and dusted her off as he glared at Walsh. They left him sitting on the floor with the other dancers laughing down at him.

He made his way over to the window and looked down into the courtyard. It was a macabre scene. In the black, empty street beyond the archway the rain still slanted down while in the harsh light of the deserted yard the three coffin-like boxes lay side by side, each with its still occupant. There was no movement from Peter or Don but Bernie opened his eyes and Walsh waved encouragingly. Bernie gave a gentle smile and raised his hand.

Reassured, Walsh turned back into the hall. He was beginning to feel better, the world had stopped whirling and he could see with both eyes. Things were going with a bang. The cabaret, provided free by the chorus girls from the Victoria Theatre down in New Town Road, was getting under way. There was a long roll on the drums, the girls kicked off their shoes and lined up, arms around each other's waists. When the music started, they moved sideways down the hall, high-kicking in unison. Many were unsteady on their feet so it was a ragged performance; but the students yelled like dervishes.

In the far corner Hugh Mills was sitting with Peter Napier's girl. His arm was along the back of her chair, his face very close to hers. He was talking steadily and it seemed he was outlining some kind of proposition because she kept shaking her head. But she was smiling: it was only a matter of time and finally she shrugged and got up. Hugh Mills, calmly possessive, ushered her across the floor and out through the door. She had nice legs and an attractive, swinging walk. Walsh thought of Peter in his coffin in the silent yard below.

The cabaret concluded to a frenzy of cheering, the girls put on their shoes and dispersed throughout the hall. One of them sat near Walsh with her escort; he was a big, beefy man in his thirties and looked like one of the hard-eyed types who inhabited the sleazy apartment houses around the college.

He was lighting a cigarette for the girl and as she bent forward her dark eyes glanced quickly at Walsh. He was feeling good and he grinned at her. She looked away immediately but he kept up his level stare, quietly waiting. After a few elaborate puffs at her cigarette she turned her eyes casually towards him. He switched on the big grin and she looked away again.

Walsh was enjoying this. He put his elbow on the back of his chair, leaned his head on his hand and kept staring. Several times her eyes were drawn round to him then rapidly away but he noticed that a corner of her mouth was beginning to twitch. Her partner, too, had seen there was a distraction; he turned and gave Walsh a hard look. Walsh ignored him and maintained his big fixed grin at the girl.

At length the man got up. 'What's the bloody big idea?' he asked, leaning over Walsh threateningly, big fists bunched. 'You bloody well trying to start something?'

Walsh, showing no sign of having heard him, continued to stare past him at the girl.

The beefy man's face flushed but he made no move. Walsh was a gaunt six foot two and his wide, bony shoulders almost gave the impression that he had forgotten to take the hanger out of his jacket. Black hair stuck out spicily above a pale, high-cheekboned face. He looked durable.

The man decided not to press the matter further and turned back to the girl; but by now she was laughing helplessly. Walsh went over to her, still ignoring her partner.

'Like to dance?' he asked and she came eagerly into his arms. They didn't speak as they went round but she pressed close and looked up at him with steady eyes and a half smile. It came to Walsh that he was wasting time.

'Come on,' he said. 'I'll show you round the building.'
She nodded without dropping her gaze and they went out
into the passage and up the stairs to the top corridor.
Students and girls were clasped tightly in every classroom
doorway. Walsh tried a few of the handles.

'No good, *chum*,' murmured a shadowy figure closely
entwined with a startling blonde. 'They're all locked.'

Right at the end was the anatomy lab. They'd probably
be able to get in there. Unsuitable in many ways but perhaps
[not] if he didn't put the light on. Anyway, it was far too
public here. They walked slowly along the corridor, her arm
around his waist, her head rolling gently on his shoulder
with each step. Her perfume came up to him and he could
feel his heart knocking against his ribs.

'In here,' he said. He turned the knob, slipped inside and
closed the door quickly behind them. In the darkness a breath
of formalin prickled in his nostrils. He felt her body stiffen.

'What's this place?' she asked.

Walsh squeezed her arm. 'Just a classroom.' He guided
her from memory between the tables with specimens.
Beyond, he knew were the tiers of forms where the lectures
were given and soon his leg rapped against a polished
wooden surface.

'This is it.' He pulled the girl down beside him and put
his arm round her bare shoulders. But she sat bolt upright,

turning her head this way and that, trying to pierce the blanketing darkness.

'I don't like it here. It smells queer. Where are we?'

'Don't be silly. I told you. It's just a classroom. Come on, relax.' He pulled her gently towards him and feeling her hair soft against his face, began to kiss her cheek. He felt her slackening in his arms; she turned and raised her mouth to him. Happily, he gathered her up and kissed her on the lips with the greatest finesse. She moaned faintly and at that moment somebody switched on the lights.

A yard away, on a metal table, lay the half dissected head of a cow. One eye had been removed and the empty socket gleamed as though a monocle had been inserted. The other regarded them incuriously while the great white mandible with its jutting teeth was fixed in a vacant grin.

As if operated by strings, the girl rose slowly from the bench, her eyes starting from her head, her mouth gaping. She took three sleepwalking steps then turned and ran.

She crashed headlong into Charlie the horse skeleton and the pride of the lab. He had always been there and the students were deeply attached to him. There was an air of peace and permanence about Charlie and he took this assault on his dignity with unruffled calm, his huge rib cage vibrating like a harp, his leg bones rattling softly in their *supporting wires. He looked down benignly on the girl and his skull gave a few reassuring nods.*

She had made no sound when she saw the cow's head but now she really found her voice and a dreadful terrified yell welled from her. She put both hands on top of her head and began to rush about among the tables filled with the specimens in readiness for tomorrow's demonstrations. Grisly portions of dogs and cats lay everywhere and right in the centre a large pig rested on its back, its legs raised quietly towards the roof.

The girl staggered from table to table, getting a bit more power into each scream till she found the door and fled through it with a last despairing cry.

Alf's girlfriends were rather less 'fast' than Walsh's chorus girl; his first date since the catastrophe at the cinema was Nan Elliot, whom he'd met at school. Another college-era girlfriend was Charlotte Clarke ('The sweetest thing I have ever known' – until she gave him the elbow), whom he met on a Boys' Brigade weekend. Another girlfriend, Marion Grant, he encountered doing some wholesome camping and hill-walking. Otherwise the fictionalization of that evening was light. 'Bernie Hill' was actually Alf's old Yoker friend, Alex Taylor, who did indeed stagger to a college dance with a Johnny Walker cut-out as a trophy, and was quite astonishingly inebriated. Dominic Boyce, prone to solitary singing when drunk in the pub and then sleeping for the main event, was the model for Don Noyce. 'Theatricals' such as chorus girls were sometime attendees at Buccleuch Street 'dos', but then the vet college dances attracted everybody in the environs of Garnethill, including dental students, cookery students, the prostitutes from the brothel opposite and the students from the Art School. The local papers liked to turn up to the Friday dances too, finding them colourful copy. A minor problem with Alf's nights out was that his mother was convinced that he was saintly close to teetotalism, which required him walking the streets for hours afterwards to sober up. Or getting his friend Eddie Straiton, the dark-haired, teetotal fitness fanatic from Clydeside, to stick his fingers down his (Alf's) throat to make him sick. Lest his mother should read it, in his diary he was careful in his recounting of the more lively events at vet college, such as a rugger trip to Edinburgh to play the Royal Dick:

> *What a journey home! Most of the lads were a trifle happy and some definitely tight. Chips, chocolate and beer went lavishly in the compartment ... More fish and chips and singing in Glasgow and I staggered in at 1 o'clock. Great stuff. P.S 'staggered' doesn't indicate any state of intoxication.*

Alf was also in the Glasgow Veterinary College football team, along with many of his best friends, including Eddie Straiton, Jimmy Steele, Bob 'Ginger' Smith, Vincent O'Reilly, Johnny Ogg, Adam

Farrell, Donald MacIntyre and Aubrey Melville. Once, after raising £16-15s-0d at a college dance, the team set off across the Irish Sea to play Dublin Veterinary College at Dalyneux Park. Excepting captain Eddie Straiton, the Glasgow team drank on the boat and drank in Dublin. They got no sleep, they played in wet kit (some wag had trailed the kit bags in the sea) yet still managed to be 3-1 up at full time. Alas, the referee, Dublin's Professor of Parasitology, kept the game going. The Glasgow boys could run no more, and when the Dubliners equalized 3-3 the ref immediately blew the *final* final whistle.

On getting back to Glasgow, Alf wrote up the Dublin outing as a short story. He showed it to, among others, Eddie Straiton, who thought it 'bloody marvellous'. Alf then put it in a drawer.

While he was at College, Alf also turned out for Yoker Fernlea in the Scottish Juvenile League, where neither the game nor the pitches – which were usually ash, gravel or mud – were beautiful. Many of the crowd at Juvenile soccer games were tribal 'gentry of the corner' who liked to trip up the opposition with a quick thrust of a leg from the touchline. It was a mistake to win away; when Yoker Fernlea crossed the Clyde on the boxy black Renfrew Ferry to trounce Govan, the local supporters attacked the Yoker team who had to barricade themselves in a shed until the police arrived. That was Alf's last game for Yoker. He played a few games for Old Kilpatrick Amateurs in the West of Scotland Amateur League, and played for the college but never again for Yoker.

There was a sort of extra time, however, for football in Alf's life. Based on his experience with Yoker Fernlea, Alf wrote an unpublished short story about a man in a Juvenile League crowd who is persuaded to turn out for an under-manned team, and who is almost destroyed by the inner conflict and physical exertions the 90 minutes bring. Although Alf had made the decision to prioritize animals over writing, he clearly had not abandoned the word. And football, Alf would find as a practising vet, was a lingua franca between him and the client, an ice-breaking topic, a means of bonding.

* * *

By Christmas 1936, Alf had broken the back of the veterinary course, having passed the professional exams in Chemistry, Physics, Physiology, Histology and Embryology, and Animal Husbandry (Animal Management). He was thrumming along too in Senior Anatomy, Pharmacology and Veterinary Hygiene. However, with the exception of Animal Husbandry – which covered everything from fitting a harness to a horse to shoeing, from manipulation to assessing conformation (body shape) – the work had been largely theoretical. That was about to change.

MR HERRIOT'S CASEBOOK

'Try her with a kipper.'

Advice of J. J. McDowall MRCVS to client

with a cat 'off her food'

It was a requirement of the MRCVS diploma that students received practical experience with professional veterinary practitioners, which was then written up as 'casebooks' to be presented for the final examination. At Glasgow, however, seeing service with working vets had an additional impetus, because the college did not have a clinic where students could prod and ponder sick animals.

So the Buccleuch Street students were assigned early and often from their third year onwards to various vets for some real hands-on sessions. The sheer amount of practical experience Glasgow students undertook was the other reason why Glasgow students were particularly sought after in the profession.

One of the first practitioners Alf spent time with was William Weipers, a Buccleuch Street old boy (and eventually its Dean), who ran a surgery in the city's fashionable West End. Sticking a finger into the trade winds, Weipers had divined the change of direction towards small animal work and had decided to specialize in pets. His practice had X-ray machines – this, at a time when human hospitals struggled to get them – and metal tables with adjustable tops in the operating theatre. Weipers' surgery was a white and steel vision of the future. Alf Wight, aspiring dog doctor, loved it. 'It was just dogs and cats all day long ... one thought hammered in my head. This is what I would do some day.'

In Glasgow, Alf also saw practice with Willie Robb, who was famed for his equine expertise. (When not toiling in his own veterinary practice, Robb doubled as a professor of Medicine and Surgery at Buccleuch Street.) But Alf went further afield than Glasgae in his search for veterinary know-how. He did a session with Donald Campbell of Rutherglen, although the most memorable aspect of the stint was not animal but human: it was Campbell's idiosyncratic habit of telephoning the 'ha-ouse' at the end of evening surgery to let his wife know he was on the way home, bawling 'I'll be leaving na-ow, I'll be na-ow' into the black mouthpiece. When Alf brought Aubrey Melville along to witness this strange ritual, Melville had to rush off and was found rolling on the floor, almost unable to breathe because of laughter.

During his vacations in 1937, Alf travelled down to the swelling hills, stony rivers, stone walls and open fields of Dumfries in south-west Scotland to see practice with Tom Fleming. Fleming's was a classic country practice, where the veterinary year was marked by spring calving and lambing, and another bout of calving in the autumn. There were few phones, fewer cars and the 'veet' was the conduit to the outside world, to be sat down on arrival and pumped for the latest news of neighbours and nation. Along with the vicar, the vet was a pastoral figure. In rural practices in the Thirties – even up to the Fifties – the relationship between vet and client was different to today, more intimate. 'Being a vet then,' recalled Herefordshire vet Nigel Carter,

> was very much a social thing and after you'd done your work on the farm you would invariably go in and wash your hands and they would say, 'Will you have a cup of tea or a piece of cake?' So there would be a quarter or half an hour socialising and you became friends more or less ... In those days people didn't travel very much or get out and the local vet calling in was how they got all the news.

The vet also doubled as the doctor, and was quite likely to be called upon to treat skin diseases of children with gentian violet, set broken limbs or pull teeth. Many a country woman quietly ordered some udder cream for her chapped hands. A Gypsy client of Nigel Carter's wanted some skin cream for an irritation on his arm. To get around any embarrassment or impropriety, Carter gave him some ointment 'for your dog'.

Doctors had their uses though; the X-ray machine in the local hospital was handy to check for a fracture of Rover's leg.

On his travels around Dumfries with Fleming in an unreliable car (vet's cars were always unreliable), Alf opened the farm gate (the student's job, always) to a caseload that was headed by cows, followed by horses, with the pig, goat and sheep as distant finishers. The relatively small number of sheep cases was a reflection of the fact that Dumfries was cattle country but also the smallness of the value of the sheep; calling out the vet and paying for medicine was likely to be more than the animal was worth.

This was a primitive landscape of small farms, carrying 15 or so cows, Ayrshires, Galloways or Shorthorns. The Ayrshire (or Dunlop) is a dual-purpose breed, producing both milk and beef, as is the Shorthorn, the subject of the first pedigree herd book in the world, *Coates's Herd Book* of 1822. The Galloway, a beast for beef, is one of the oldest breeds of cattle in Britain. Alf wanted to see cows in Dumfries and he saw them. Herds of them on a single day:

Monday 22 March 1937

1. *Cow calved last Wed. Retained cleansings. Taking food all right. Uterus contracted thus allowing only two fingers to work with. Cleansings removed & 2 boric*

acid & methyl violet pessaries inserted. Keep on bran mashes with little food. Little cake allowed. Rug up. Let out a while in first spell of good weather.

2. *Cow cleansed by Mr F. Last week – not doing so well. Off her food. Syphoned off fluid then irrigated with pump. Usual pessaries. Also foal with rheumatism.*

3. *Cleansed cow – as usual. Castrated two calves – bloodless. To return if testicles not shrivelled after 6–8 weeks. Cord merely crushed. Gave farmer stomach powder for cow – Ammon Carb, Nux Vom, ginger.*

4. *Cow off feed, shivering, fever, quick, shallow stirterous [sic: stertorous] rasping.*

Diagnosis – pneumonia, due to standing in stall opposite door in badly ventilated bire. Mustard on chest walls, covered by newspapers, then rugs. Injection of hexamine (unable to do so intravenously owing to struggling). Cow then drenched with 8 pints Aeth. Lit., Ammon Aect. in milk. Hexamine was heated first.

Struggling cows were a perennial problem in the lot of the country vet in the Thirties, before the 'crush', a metal cage, was invented to immobilize cattle for treatment. Theoretically a cow could be 'cast' (put on its back or side) with ropes, one method being that described in *Black's Veterinary Dictionary*, 1928:

> *For casting cattle a common method is to make a running*
> *noose in one end of a long rope (30 feet at least), and pass*
> *this round the bases of the horns or round the neck in polled*
> *cattle (for the latter the noose should be fixed instead of*
> *running to avoid choking). A half-hitch is next made round*
> *the neck, a second round the chest immediately behind the*
> *elbows, and a third round the abdomen in front of the*
> *udder or scrotum.*

When the rope was pulled on, the cow would sink to the ground, at which point one person would secure the cow by kneeling on its neck and another would tie the cow's feet to a fence or wagon.

Casting a cow was deuced tricky to do, however, because Daisy first had to be persuaded to stand still. Some tame cows might be tied standing up with a halter, but as Alf discovered with Tom Fleming, 'tame' is a relative state in bovines. On one unforgettable day, his arms lathered with soap, Alf attempted to 'cleanse a cow' and cautiously tugged at the mass of wine-dark afterbirth hanging from the rear end of the handily tethered Galloway. At this assault upon her person the Galloway trumpeted her indignation and determined upon escape through a window in the shed. Alas the window was tiny, the cow was big, and as she burst through the opening she took the end off the shed. Amidst the collapsed timbers Alf Wight, Tom Fleming and the farmer watched the cow, part of the shed stuck round her neck, hoofing it for the horizon. 'Let the bugger go!' exclaimed the farmer.

The tendency of the temperamental Galloway to charge anything on two legs was one reason why farmers had bred the beastie to be hornless. Farmers are no fools: better a charging 400 kg Galloway without horns than a charging 400 kg Galloway with them. Vets are no fools either; some, when required to inject Galloways with calcium boro-gluconate against milk fever stabbed the needle into the hide, then ran to the car, in which the engine had been left running.

Still, temper or not, the Galloway was (and is) a good breed for Scottish farms with rough or hill pasture because of its preternatural ability to convert poor grazing into good beef, and all this without being fed expensive cattle cake in the long cold winter months.

The vet's standard wear on farm work was a brown smock, but for calving and cleansing, stripping off to the waist was usual. In winter in a shed high on the hills, at least the work kept the chill off. 'I was the only one who was warm,' Nigel Carter remembered of a night when it was cold enough to freeze his veterinary instruments to the tray, 'because the work was warm – and it was warm inside the cow too.' Since few farms had electricity, the farmer or farm worker – or student vet – had to hold a tilly lamp. *He* would shiver, and so shake the light, making it difficult to see properly.

Alf came to love cows, and when he moved to Thirsk he would become the 'cow doctor' to Donald Sinclair's 'horsey man'. It is just as well Alf loved cows because there was plenty more to do with them in Dumfries. There were cows whose feet needed to be pared, bullocks to be dishorned ('Used dishorning shears. Great haemorrhage. Dressed with boric acid afterwards. Sufficient chloroform was given to induce dullness') and cows to be post-mortemed.

J. A. Wight Casebook 1937:

Post-mortem on Ayrshire cow.

There were innumerable small, hard caseous nodules in the lungs & in the bronchial & mediastinal glands. There were similar lesions, though fewer in number, in the liver & kidneys. The udder was also slightly affected.

Diagnosis: Miliary tuberculosis

Another post-mortemed cow, this one with 'oedematous swellings', was found to have eaten wire, which had worked its way from the stomach into the thoracic cavity. Wire was used to tie hay and straw bales, and broken bits of wire bindings were consumed by cows with a fatal regularity.

As Alf would observe in *The Lord God Made Them All*, 'A lot of time was spent pouring things down cows' throats' in the

Thirties. Universal Cattle Medicine ('Never Fails to Give Relief') was a favourite drench for bovines, at least among farmers, because the camphor-ammonia produced a jolt when sniffed, and 'made farmers blink and shake their heads and say, "By gaw, that's powerful stuff," with deep respect.'

Drenching cows was always easier said than done. Over in Snowdonia, however, farmer Thomas Firbank saw two neighbours give a veritable masterclass in the art of pouring liquid down a cow's throat:

> The youth had his arm over the cow's neck, grasping a horn, and his other hand was twisting up the cow's head by a firm grip on the nose, a finger in each nostril. His father dextrously inserted the tip of a hollow horn in the animal's mouth, and poured down a mixture which smelled of aniseed. The cow gurgled, and when released coughed a little, with the impersonal passivity which raises a cow so far above the frailties of human passion.

Actually, quite a lot of time on farms in the Thirties was spent squirting things (notably antiseptic Acriflavine) into *every* available orifice of cows and other beasts. So Alfie saw in Dumfries: pails of hot salt water pumped into stomach tubes to treat horse colic; a cow's vagina douched with 10 grams of iodine crystals in a pint of water with 'pot. iod.'; a mare's urinary passage washed out by Higginson's syringe; a cow with an infected uterus pumped with five gallons of water containing ½ lb of common salt; and a light draught gelding with 'weed' (lymphangitis) treated with 2 gallons of water with 2 lbs of sodium chloride.

The cure for milk fever, though, was neither drench nor douche. It was an injection with a hypodermic needle, as Alf dutifully recorded in his casebook.

> *Cow, 9 years old. Calved Saturday. Staring eyes, costive, staggering on rising. Diagnosis: Milk fever. Treatment: Injection of 3oz of calcium borogluconate. Instructions to give no food today & light feeding afterwards. To give 2 or 3 lbs of treacle to relieve constipation. Stomach powder also given (Glucose & sod. Bicarb).*

Beating milk fever, a disease of lactating cows, was one of veterinary medicine's great pre-War triumphs. A Danish vet, Jurgens Schmidt, had discovered by trial and error that pumping potassium iodide into an affected cow's teats worked a sort of cure, before another Danish vet found that pumping in air was equally effective. At Edinburgh University, Dryerre and Greig divined that milk fever was caused by loss of calcium – pressure from pumping was effective because it halted the flow of milk and that replacing calcium loss by an injection of calcium borogluconate was the actual practical answer.

Of course, inflation of the udder would still do the trick of curing milk fever, but a hypodermic syringe had a considerably more professional image than a bicycle pump.

Since an injection of calcium boroglucanate seemed a wonder cure, it was used by Tom Fleming in hope and desperation on all sorts of improbable patients, such as calves with pneumonia.

Some of Tom Fleming's methods of diagnosis were admirably straightforward, as Alf recorded on a visit to a sick horse:

History: Had grown lame in off hind leg. Since there was an abrasion on the pastern, the owner suspected tetanus. The horse therefore had been doing little work & yet receiving the normal oat ration.

Examination: temp 103°F

The horse was struck smartly under the chin and there was no sign of the third eyelid – thus eliminating the possibility of tetanus.

An Ayrshire cow also received the physical treatment. 'Her responses were all right as demonstrated when a knife was inserted between the clit [hooves].'

Fleming's methods may have sometimes lacked finesse but they were sound and conscientious. Diagnosis was the vet's forte in the Thirties. It was just a pity about the limitations of the cures.

Even a country practice like Tom Fleming's was seeing more and more pets, particularly dogs, on the client list as the Thirties wore on. Like everything else in the world, dog breeds go in fashions: Pekingese, Spaniels and Fox Terriers headed the Thirties must-have list and Labradors, today's most popular breed, were far less sought after.

The Pekingese, it might be said, was the vet's best financial friend. One of the world's oldest dog breeds, dating back to 2000 BC, the Pekingese had long been the exclusive property of the Chinese imperial family; it had been introduced into Britain in 1860 following the occupation of Peking at the end of the Second Opium War, when five of the dogs belonging to the Empress Dowager Ci'an were found in the sacked Summer Palace and shipped west. Queen Victoria had received one of the plundered Pekes (which she had archly named 'Looty'), so keeping the breed's connection to royalty and matrons. By 1904 the Pekingese breed had become sufficiently established for the Pekingese Club of England to be founded, and ten years later it had become the most popular dog breed in the Western world, loved for its loyalty and dignity.

The Pekingese – believed in Chinese legend to be the result of a mating between a lion and a monkey – is also wilful, obstinate and dominant. As the American writer Dorothy Parker acidly observed: 'No woman who owns that lily of the field, a Pekingese, can be accused of selfishness. She simply hasn't the time to think of herself. His Serene Highness demands unceasing attention.'

The Peke can also require much attention from the veterinary profession, because it has a hereditary disposition to respiratory and eye ailments. It also tends towards alimentary illnesses when overfed, which it frequently is, being so often the spoiled lap dog, or baby substitute, of the Mrs Pumphreys of the world.

There were definite shades of Tricky-Woo, ruler of Mrs Pumphrey in Thirsk, in almost every encounter Fleming had with a Peke. On 31 August Alf entered in his casebook:

History: Previously visited & found to be exhibiting symptoms of vesical calculi. Cystotomy had been advised.

Operative procedure: The bitch, after being prepared by morphia injection, was anaesthetized by pumping air through a bottle containing chloroform. She had previously been secured to the four corners of the table by hobbles. After the hair had been removed from the abdominal wall, the site of operation was bathed with iodo-benzol. The abdomen was then wrapped in surgical gauze & the first incision made through the gauze. On reaching the bladder a ¾" incision was made & 33 calculi of various sizes removed by expression. The site was kept clear by continuous use of swabs. The incision on the bladder was closed by means of two layers of continuous suture, the second layer burying the first, thus preventing leakage. The skin incision was then closed by interrupted sutures.

The bitch was then put in her pen, and put on a regimen of a 'few laps' of water only for a day or two. A week later, Fleming and Alf treated an 11-month old Pekingese bitch, which was 'continually scratching and biting' at the root of its tale. This was discovered to be suffering from impacted anal glands – what Mrs Pumphrey would rather more charmingly call 'flop-bot' – which were duly evacuated by manipulation. Since the irritated skin was likely caused by a worm infestation, Fleming prescribed a 24-hour fast and anthelmintic pill. If ineffectual, a 'dose of castor oil' was to be administered.

Another Pekingese was urinating frequently and on palpitation calculi were found in the bladder, and a cystorectomy advised; another Pekingese bitch had an ascitis and was treated by an incision into the abdominal wall and the dropsical fluid run off; an eight-year-old Pekingese dog visited had a growth on the dorsal surface of the left hind paw, which Fleming diagnosed as a papilloma and excised, after anaesthetizing the part with novocaine.

Women were overwhelmingly Peke owners in the Thirties, as Hollywood drolly reflected in the character of dizzy socialite Angela Bullock in the 1936 screwball comedy *My Man Godfrey*, and in Trixie Lorraine in the Busby Berkeley musical, the *Golddiggers* of 1933. But Wire Fox Terriers also stole the scene, led by Asta the sniffer-out of corpses and clues on behalf of Nick and Nora Charles in the *Thin Man* detective films and Snowy, the travelling companion of Tin Tin. Asta and Snowy sparked a veritable craze for Wire Fox Terriers, which is why they were such a regular item on Fleming and Alf's client list.

A visit to an 'off colour' Fox Terrier pointed up a real problem with keeping a dog in the hard times of the Thirties. The dog 'had been receiving very little meat, its diet consisting largely of biscuits', which in turn had caused eczema. Fleming advised bathing the dog in warm water medicated with derris root, with 'liquor arsenicalis' to be taken internally. He added that 'more meat' was to be given in the canine's diet. Most vets had an unofficial sliding scale of charges, but pet owners who could not afford even the vet's lowest fee might find a local branch of the People's Dispensary for Sick Animals, the veterinary charity founded by Marie Dickin in 1917.

Some of the cases Alf saw with Tom Fleming were heartbreaking, reminders that one of the worst aspects of a vet's life (and one of the reasons that vets are prone to depression) is that the job entails the killing of animals. A Scotch Terrier with tumours was destroyed 'on owner's instructions' by 'choloroform inhalation (1oz. in mask)'; a cross-bred dog with chronic nephritis or Stuttgart's disease 'too advanced to have any hope of recovery' was destroyed by injection of prussic acid; a Springer Spaniel was likewise killed by injection of prussic acid on 23 March 1937, Alf writing in his casebook:

Destroyed dog. Spaniel 14 years old. Smelling strongly. Teeth bad. Growth on nose, & eyes & tumour at base of tail. Prussic acid into thoracic cavity, quick panting respirations, barks, then a howl. Slight convulsion.

Down the years, the relief given to the Labrador seen on 28 August 1937 is almost palpable:

Labrador-retriever dog, 8 months old.

History – had previously been treated for hysteria which had been evidenced by occasional fits of barking, running eye. 'Luminal' had been given, the result being unsatisfactory.

Treatment: a rectal injection of warm soapy water was made producing evacuation of considerable amount of faeces. 3ozs of liquid paraffin was given, producing further evacuation

in 12 hours. A worm capsule was then administered.

In the Thirties, 'knackeries' or 'knacker's yards' sprinkled the British farming countryside, being the places where fallen livestock were carted to be processed. The knackery was a Brueghelian world: heaps of dead decomposing animals lay all over the yard, most in some state of dismemberment, as the knacker bled them, stripped them of their skin, and took out their bones and bowels. Here buckets of blood, there a mound of shiny intestines, everywhere the suffocating stench of carcasses being boiled. In the corners awaiting collection, a pile of bleached bones and skulls (to be turned into fertilizer) and a mound of fly-covered meat for the cat or dog food shop in town.

It was a unique learning environment, if a gruesome one, for a vet in training like Alf. On a visit to a knackery in 1937, he saw, in the flesh, a version of colic that was untreatable, torsion of the intestine, or twisted bowel. Alf's first solo case in Thirsk would be a hunter with colic, and not just any old hunter but one of Lord Fulton's best hunters, as his lordship's manager so unpleasantly pointed out. Those hands-on hours with Tom Fleming would help Alf diagnose a torsion and firm his resolve to put the horse out of pain.

Knackeries were a sight not easily forgotten. Or stomached. On his first visit to the knackers in Dumfries, Alf did what every first visitor to the knackers did. He spewed up his breakfast. This was much to the amusement of the knacker's man sitting on a carcase, a sandwich in one blood-stained hand, a teacup in the other. Surrounded by pretty much every disease known to animalkind, the knacker's mate was a pink-skinned advert for health, when common sense said he should be pale, wheezing and ailing. As a breed, though, knackers were conspicuously hale and hearty, the proof being Jeff Mallock and his family, whom Alf encountered on moving to Thirsk. In the Mallock's family bungalow, which was plop in the middle of their yard, lived cherubic Jeff, his comely wife, and a family which ranged from a beautiful girl of nineteen down to feisty boy of five. 'There were eight young Mallocks, and they spent their lifetimes playing among tuberculous lungs and a vast spectrum of bacteria from Salmonella to Anthrax. They were the healthiest children in the district.'

Aside from knackers and their kin, everyone else in the British countryside lived in dread of tuberculosis, which went by an array of names, sometimes being consumption, the Great White Plague, Piner's Disease, Grapes or Phthisis. However termed, the disease made up a large proportion of the vet's workload in the inter-war period because infected cattle could transmit the disease to humans via milk and flesh. In 1934 alone, there were 2500 human deaths in Britain from bovine TB; it was the vet's job to determine whether cattle were 'TB'-free by testing, which was done by injecting tuberculin, a solution of the poisons of tubercle bacilli, into the skin along the cow's neck or into the skin at the fold of the tail. A positive reaction, meaning that tuberculosis was present, would be evidenced by a swelling of the skin up to the size of a walnut.

In 1931, 15 per cent of the dairy herds that supplied Glasgow were discovered to be contaminated with TB, and possibly as many as 33,000 of Scotland's 450,000 dairy cows and heifers were infected. Perhaps not surprisingly, then, Glasgow had the highest death rate from TB in the country before the Second World War. Under the government's 1925 Tuberculosis Order, all farmers who suspected their cattle of having TB were instructed to notify the local authority. Many ignored the injunction because the compensation was £3 a head whereas the cow's market value was more like £12. Farmers peddled on cows that were not yet showing definite clinical signs of the disease.

Milk could be deadly, a white soup of bacteria causing typhoid, scarlet fever, listeria and salmonella, as well as TB. The milking machines, which were replacing hand milking, if anything spread infection. To ensure production of safer milk, the government's Milk Order of 1922 provided a scheme whereby 'Milk may be graded and supplied under certain conditions of comparative bacteriological purity.'

Three premium grades of milk were introduced – Grade A (Tuberculin Tested); Grade A (Pasteurized); Grade A – the definition was whether the herd was tuberculosis-free, what other diseases might be present, and whether the milk was pasteurized or raw.

All the rest of Britain's milk was 'non-graded'. The difference in price between ungraded and Grade A was a significant 1d a pint. Hardly anyone could afford to buy it, and therefore farmers did not think the effort of producing it worthwhile. About 1 per cent of milk drunk in the early Thirties was Grade A. Not until the Milk Marketing Board introduced a 1d premium per gallon to the farmer did supplies take off and consumption increase.

A vet received £20 per day from the government for undertaking TB testing, and most were desperate for the work. A routine day's work in a mixed practice usually garnered £2–3. Founded in 1897, the Veterinary Benevolent Fund to aid destitute vets received tens of begging letters a day in the Thirties. A common reason for the destitution of vets, aside from the poor economics of veterinary medicine, was that the work could make them ill, and therefore unable to work.

* * *

Doc Whitehouse had promised Alf that veterinary surgery contained variety, if not money, and it did. On 24 March 1937 alone, Alf attended a ewe with her placenta out, a lamb with incurable 'joint ill', a cow that required irrigation ('ineffectual') to remove cleansings, a dog with an abscess on its jaw ('cut out & pus liberated'), a Dalmatian puppy with hysteria that the owner wanted destroyed (Fleming refused), a calving case (Fleming got the calf out and tried to induce breathing by pressing on thoracic walls but the animal died), and lastly a mare suffering peritonitis.

In between his case work with Fleming, Alf also had to slog away at Buccleuch Street at Senior Anatomy, Pharmacology and Hygiene, and he made very good progress in all of them. Sitting the professional exams in July 1937, he passed with 45 (Senior Anatomy), 57 (Pharmacology) and 56 per cent (Hygiene) respectively. So, it was on to the fourth year of study: Pathology, Parasitology, and Medicine and Surgery. Pathology, of course, was taught by the dreaded Emslie, who entered into the student report book at the end of the autumn term under the name J. A. Wight: 'Attendance good … Pleasant manner.' The killer detail came in the middle, though: 'Performance rather poor.' In the spring term of 1938, Alf improved, but it was not going to be a surprise to either Emslie or Alf that the latter was 'referred Pathology' in the professional examination in July 1938 with a mark of 40 per cent. Having failed to conquer Pathology, Alf went off and summitted Streap mountain near Loch Arkaig in broiling weather. He and Pathology were to be closely acquainted for another year yet.

Just as he had roamed the hills as a boy, he roamed them as a student, going camping almost every weekend from Easter to October, 'leaving the smoke and dirt of Glasgow behind us' as

Alf expressed it in *Vets Might Fly*. Loch Lomond was a regular venue, where the beauty of the birch-lined shore at Rowardennan made sufficient an impression on Alf that he later named his house in Yorkshire after it. His other favourite place to pitch a tent was Rosneath on a peninsula in the Firth of Clyde, where Alf found a 'fairyland which led me into the full wonder and beauty of the world'.

Such were the demands of studying for the MRCVS diploma, however, that Alf had to always sherpa his textbooks with him on his hill jaunts, so he could swot in the sun and cram under canvas in the rain.

* * *

In 1938 Chamberlain returned from his Munich meeting with Hitler promising 'Peace in our Time', and 13,500,000 people attended the Empire Exhibition (Scotland) at Bellhouston Park, and the whole of Britain danced away to the sound of 'The Lambeth Walk'. It was also the year Alf saw practice with a vet in Sunderland, a vet who was to become friend, eventual employer and, disguised as boozing Angus Grier, a character in the Herriot gallery. This was J. J. McDowall, whose surgery was handily just around the corner from Alf's Auntie Jinny Wilkins on Beechwood Terrace. In Jock McDowall's suburban Sunderland practice, dogs and cats were the bread and butter. Or, as McDowall, brick-red of face, hot of temper, with a clipped-colonel moustache and colourful tongue put it, 'The folk around here will rush their pet to me at the drop of a hat. They're in through the door if it coughs, sneezes or farts!' He even had customers willing to pay 5 shillings for the vaccine against canine distemper, an almost miraculous advance in veterinary medicine, but the cost of which was judged prohibitive by most dog-owners.

And, truly, not many vets of the time performed an ovariotomy on a cat. Alf wrote in his casebook that year:

The cat was anaesthetised [and] The site of operation (the flank) was clipped, shaved and rubbed with iodine. An incision (1½ inches long) was made through skin and two layers of muscle. The final incision through the deepest layer of muscle was only ½ inch long. The ovary was sought (recognised by colour and shape) and seized by forceps & drawn out through the incision. A pair of artery forceps was clipped over the horn of the uterus and another over the ovarian vessels. Ligature were applied and the horn of the uterus & the vessels were severed.

McDowall then inserted sutures and covered the area in antiseptic dusting powder before repeating the procedure for the other ovary. The cat was then swaddled in pads of cotton wool and bandages.

When the cat was visited a week later the wounds were clean and healing nicely. Unfortunately, the cat was not taking any food.

McDowall's unflappable advice was 'try her with a kipper'.

One of McDowall's mottos was, 'It's not what you do, it's the way that you do it.' If in doubt, with dogs he diagnosed 'hysteria' (caused by some combination of 'teething, worms, gastric problems') and prescribed a sedative, a wormer and 'keeping the bowels open'.

Like veterinary practices everywhere, the caseload Nature provided for treatment at 1 Thornhill Terrace, McDowall's surgery, was only increased by the stupidities of humans. One farmer who should have known better called in the 'v'itnry' to look at a black-faced ewe. Alf's casebook recorded that the ewe:

> Had developed a swelling on the left side of the face which had been thought to be an abscess.

> Examination: The swelling had been caused simply by an accumulation of grass between the lower molar teeth & the left cheek. This was removed.

Following an appointment to see a Cocker Spaniel, Alf entered in his casebook:

History: The owner had been dosing the animal somewhat drastically for worms & yesterday the animal had had a 'fit'. He was off his food and occasionally vomiting...

Diagnosis: gastric ulcer. The fit was caused by the pain consequent on the administration of a 'soap fill'.

McDowall put the Cocker Spaniel on a milky diet, with regular doses of a stomach and sedative mixture. More tragic was the case of another Cocker Spaniel, who was suffering a dislocated hip after a road accident; unfortunately the dog had been 'treated by a quack' for several days, who had made bad matters worse. 'Had the dog been brought in shortly after the accident,' Alf wrote, 'it would have been a fairly easy matter to replace the dislocation but it was now too late to do anything & destruction was advised.'

In Scotland, so the saying goes, the weather is so variable that you can have four seasons in one day. In veterinary surgery, equally, you can have all the emotional seasons in the space of 24 hours. On the very same day McDowall and Alf revisited a Bull Terrier bitch that had been scalded, her skin turning badly eczemous, a fortnight before. Time and McDowall's treatment of a spirit dressing (metholated spirits, antiseptic powder and a little iodine) had worked wonders, with the vile crust falling off to 'leave mostly normal skin'. Of course, such spirits-raising victories were all the better when they came quickly, as with a one-year-old Sealyham bitch, which was refusing to eat and showing evidence of pain. McDowall carefully palpated the dog's stomach, at which the 'bitch showed pain on pressure exerted'. McDowall's diagnosis was that the dog had 'swallowed a long piece of bone which had become lodged, probably in pyloric end of stomach'. The next day, after being prescribed a stomach mixture, made up principally of calcium magnesite, the bitch vomited up said bone. 'Recovery followed.' McDowall's dexterity with his hands, which was typical of vets in the Thirties, was then demonstrated in the whelping of a Scotch Terrier bitch, with McDowall exploring the bitch's vagina 'by means of one finger carefully inserted', and discovering a pup with an abnormally large head. This was extricated with forceps, and the rest of the litter popped out to round off another successful case.

The nearby South Shields greyhound track, where McDowall was 'veterinary surgeon in attendance' provided many of their patients, some of them hapless, including one dog that had stubbed its toe and another that 'had been running & collided with another dog'. Modern greyhound racing, with an oval track and a mechanical hare, was a new sport in Britain. The first meeting of the Greyhound Racing Association had taken place at Belle Vue Stadium, Manchester, on 24 July 1926, when 1700 people watched six races of seven greyhounds. A year later Belle Vue was attracting 70,000 per meeting and the GRA had stakes in 18 tracks around Britain. 'Going to the dogs' was firmly established as a proletarian spectator sport. With all the money exchanging hands in betting on greyhound racing, the potential for malpractice became evident. In 1928 the National Greyhound Racing Club was set up to establish and enforce a set of rules for racing – which is where the vets came in.

Aside from tending to injured dogs, the course vet had to ensure that dogs were fit to race, and had not been doped, overfed or otherwise nobbled. Alf's experiences at South Shield's dog track were later transposed to Yorkshire in *Vets Might Fly*. Villains in camel coats with bottle-blonde girlfriends, crooked officials, George Formby blaring on the speakers, abuse from owners whose dogs he rightly disqualified, shifty-eyed punters staring at the race card, loitering local gangsters in black suits with their overdressed girlfriends in tow – such were the joys of a day at the dog races for a young vet. The only friendliness Alf found was a pitying bookie, who saw his frayed shirt and tossed him half a crown.

Alf did not spend all his time at 1 Thornhill Terrace merely assisting Jock McDowall. The Veterinary Surgeons Act, which prohibited the practice of veterinary medicine by the non-qualified, was a full decade away, so J. J. McDowall MRCVS frequently went off, leaving plain J. A. Wight Esq. to run the shop. All by himself. Alf wrote to his parents in 1938 from Sunderland:

Down at the clinic (where Wight is in charge) I had to remove a tumour from a dog aged 12 years and after hacking away for a bit found it was attached to a testicle – so I had to remove the testicle too ... I can tell you, I wished Mac had been by my side. I sent the dog away with a horrible wound and never expected to see it alive again. Strange to say, it turned up for dressing two days later, bright and frisky and the wound beautifully clean. I felt immensely bucked up about it.

The 'clinic' was the downstairs of McDowall's house; like almost all vets he lived above the shop. Aside from cutting overheads, living on the premises cut the distance from bed to the dispensary when patience-trying calls came at two in the morning.

Eleven of the 77 cases Alf saw with McDowall involved horses, most of them working animals. Although McDowall's practice covered some of the small dairy farms on Sunderland's outskirts, the horses on the list were mostly pullers of milk floats, beer wagons and coal carts. And most of the damage done to them was human-inflicted. In his casebook on 12 April 1938, Alf recorded a visit to a heavy draught gelding that 'had strained himself over a heavy load & had been since lame'. On examination, the stifle and hip appeared to be swollen, and when pressure was applied to the hip 'the animal evinced pain'. McDowall considered that the injury was so severe that it 'would be useless to attempt heat treatment or massage with liniment', and the only possible cure was 'a year at grass'. Three days later Mac and Alf visited another lame draught horse. This time the injury had been caused by 'bad driving'. Fortunately, the injury was not severe and McDowall's advice was to hose the shoulder with cold water and get a better fitting collar. And 'to change the driver'.

But J. J. McDowall was a man of eminent sense and practicality. Attending a farm, Mac was asked to insert a ring in a bullock's nose. Alf's casebook noted that the animal was 'restrained by means of a rope round the horns', this held by a farmhand inside the stall with the bullock. Meanwhile, McDowall 'standing on the other side of the gate' – out of harm's way, in other words – stuck pincers into the bullock's nose, removed a piece of cartilage and placed in the ring. And left the farmhand and the sore-nosed bullock to it.

Alf did not enter *everything* he learned with McDowall in his student casebook of 1938. McDowall's second unofficial motto was: 'Never make a job look too easy.' Because the client always likes to feel he or she is getting their money's worth. When a calving was going too easily, he admitted to Alf, he sometimes held the calves *in*.

Such was the Art of Veterinary Medicine.

DEAR MR FARNON

For Alf Wight and his fellow survivors at Buccleuch Street in 1939, the final professional examinations loomed at least as large, and almost as frighteningly as the gathering clouds of war.

The finals consisted of two papers: first, the Principles and Practice of Veterinary Medicine, of which the written part was three hours and the oral/practical two hours; and second, the Principles and Practice of Veterinary Surgery, of which the written part was another three hours and the oral/practical another two. At least one hour of the final practical exam was devoted to surgical applied anatomy, operative surgery and anaesthesia.

The only way to get through the necessary revision was a monkish regime of self-discipline, although Buccleuch Street student Ian Cameron perhaps took this too far. According to Eddie Straiton, Cameron

was reputed to sleep four hours in the twenty-four and start his swotting at 4 a.m. every morning. I well remember the laughter in the common room when James Herriot burst in one morning and loudly announced, 'You'll never guess lads, but how's this for conscientious swotting? Ian Cameron has cut his lavatory time down to two minutes every third day!

Straiton thought they needed Alf's humour in the spring of 1939. Glasgow Corporation had begun the distribution of anti-gas protective helmets for babies, and had taken on 1500 men to erect Anderson steel air-raid shelters in back gardens in city housing schemes. Unfortunately, when Glasgow's air-raid sirens were tested, citizens had difficulty hearing the warbling note over the traffic din.

In this final year of the course, there was only one lecture per morning, and an afternoon every second week at Glasgow meat market. Every spare second was spent at the Mitchell Library or studying at home. Eddie Straiton found the finals a ' nightmare' of stress, which left such an indelible wound on his mind that he would still awake 50 years later in a cold sweat convinced he had to re-sit them. 'When we foregathered at the Maclay Hall in Glasgow University where the written part of the examination was to be held,' he recalled,

we were a 'wabbit' looking lot. Harry Donovan had shrunk to under six stones, and another pal, a tall, wild red-haired Highlander called Maurice McMorran hadn't shaved for two months.

During the first week we faced two three-hour papers on each of four subjects – surgery, obstetrics, medicine and meat inspection – in all, forty-eight questions covering the whole of our last two years' work and a considerable portion of the other three. The papers were tricky and very difficult; it seemed obvious they were out to plough as many of us as possible.

But the worst was yet to come: ten days of orals and practical tests. In the words of the 'referred' students (those who had previously sat and failed), 'The examiners tore you to shreds in the first five minutes of the oral.' We had to endure one hour of intensive interrogation on each subject.

As we waited our turn the loos were overworked; some lads were sick. How we managed to survive is a mystery. I moved automatically from one examiner to another in a mental haze as I tried to answer the endless stream of questions.

The stress in the exams was palpable, and after the exams, there was the excruciating wait for the result, hanging around the notice-board like convicts awaiting the rope. In July 1939 Alf joined the wan, worn-out students outside the ground-floor office to find he had passed Medicine but had been 'R(eferred). S(urgery)'.

Alf's father, who had never of course wanted Alf to be a vet, was devastated. No-one, however, was surprised by Alf's failure; he had just undergone a second operation at the Western Infirmary for his fistula. Jock McDowall wrote a consoling letter from Sunderland:

> *I fully expect you will have had your operation by this time and you're possibly not feeling too good. I expect the surgeon would make what is commonly called a few heroic gashes in your tender spot. You were unfortunate in getting asked all those questions about the Corpus luteum and Graafian follicles in your oral. I couldn't have said much myself about the subject. However, it says a whole lot when you sailed through Medicine. By Jove, you must have put in some graft despite not feeling too well; you deserve a medal.*

And so Alf settled down for more months of 'graft', revising Surgery over and over again. On the morning of Sunday 3 September, he took a break to listen to the radio to hear Chamberlain announce that 'this country is at war with Germany'. For the second time in Alf's life, Glasgow had a black-out at night.

In December, Alf sat Surgery again. Up went the results outside the office. Once more Alf pushed forward and scanned the list – and once more found he had failed. As he turned leadenly away, wondering how to break the bad news to his parents, the staff room door opened and Professor Whitehouse reappeared, with a piece of paper in his hand.

'My apologies, gentlemen,' said Whitehouse, as he pinned the paper to the board. 'There has been a clerical error. Another name is to be added to the list.'

The name was that of the immensely relieved J. A. Wight, dizzily gone from hope down to despair up to the very elated top of the world.

Six months later, it was Eddie Straiton's turn to await the worst. Or the best. The frail Principal Whitehouse limped from the staff room with the all-important piece of paper and gave it to Straiton to pin up.

> *My hand shook visibly … I glanced down the list and saw opposite my name the letter P. My knees turned to jelly. I was a veterinary surgeon at last.*

His joy was cut short by the cries of anguish around him; of the 127 students who had started with Straiton, only five had got through in the prescribed five years. It was the worst 'plough' in the history of Glasgow Veterinary College.

On reaching home Straiton felt ill, 'the worst reaction to acute stress I have ever known'.

Alf, before he left College, went into the office to read what the teachers had scribbled about him in the now-released confidential student reports. To his pleasurable surprise, he found that Emslie had written: 'Lacking in brilliance but showed a perception of the subject which I personally found rewarding. A pleasant-mannered, likeable boy of transparent integrity.' Alf read the lines several times, closed the book and went out through the arch of the college. He did so with a lump in his throat. 'When I qualified and walked out of the door of the college for the last time,' he wrote decades later in the introduction to *James Herriot's Dog Stories*, 'I felt an acute sense of loss, an awareness of something good gone for ever. Some of my happiest years were spent in that seedy old building and though my veterinary course was out of date and inefficient in many ways, there was a carefree, easy-going charm about that whole time which has held it in my mind in a golden glow.'

In *The Scotsman,* there appeared a notice of some pleasure and pride to Alf, Hannah and Pop Wight:

Glasgow Veterinary College (Incorporated).

The following students passed the Final Professional Examinations and Qualified MRCVS in December 1939.

Dominic Boyce. Clydebank: J. S. Deane. Glasgow: J. D. Dunn. Bearsden: A. V. Farrell. Dumfries: G. Macleod. Glasgow: M. Maclellan. North Uist: A. O. Merry. Glasgow: J. B. Milligan. Chrystom: D. J. Munro. Skye: Miss Elspeth Parker. Glasgow: Alex Shaw. Glasgow: R. T. Smith. Strathneffer: D. B. Steele. Larkhall: Miss M. C. Stevenson.

Glasgow: J. I. Tulloch. Kilmarnock: Miss M. B. Weir. Glasgow: J. A. Wight. Glasgow: R. K. Meiklem. Bishopbriggs. Wm. Burrows. Troon.

When Alf walked out into Buccleuch Street, he left some good friends behind him, some of whom would take a while yet to qualify. Although fast Eddie Straiton qualified in 1940 and Aubrey Melville passed MRCVS in a respectable December 1941, Donald McIntyre was 'Referred Surgery' five times, not finally passing MRCVS until July 1942. On failing to get his diploma in July 1939, December 1939 and July 1940, Robert Nisbet of Alf's year 'Left for HMF' (His Majesty's Forces) but came back after the war. He passed MRCVS in 1949, by which time he was 36.

When Alf walked out of the college for the last time, he also stepped into a profession on its uppers. 'Being a newly qualified veterinary surgeon ... was like taking out a ticket for a dole queue,' he recalled in *If Only They Could Talk*. 'Agriculture was depressed by a decade of government neglect, the draught horse which had been the mainstay of the profession was fast disappearing. It was easy to be a prophet of doom when the young men emerging from the colleges after five years' hard slog were faced by a world indifferent to their enthusiasm and bursting knowledge.'

Each week, the *Veterinary Record* could muster only two or three situations vacant, and there were an average of 80 applicants for each one. Most veterinary surgeons simply could not afford an assistant. Deciding that there was no near or realistic chance of working as a vet, some Glasgow veterinary graduates went to the shipyards – once more booming due to an order book from the Admiralty – as labourers, or signed on as dustmen or street cleaners. One bright lad in Straiton's year went to teach in a typing school. Straiton tried to join the army but the authorities were adamant that veterinary surgeons were a 'reserved occupation' and said a resounding 'No' to a career in khaki for Edward Straiton MRCVS.

Students lucky enough to get posts found themselves working for the chicken feed of £1-10s a week. Or less. Some qualified vets placed 'Will Work for Keep' notices in the *Record*, until an embarrassed profession asked the editor to cease publishing them.

And anyone taking a post as an assistant could expect to be little more than a dogsbody. 'Assistants were just little bits of dirt to be starved and worked into the ground by principals who were heartless and vicious to a man', Alf wrote in *If Only They Could Talk*. 'Dave Stevens, lighting a cigarette with trembling hand: "Never a night off or a half day. He made me wash the car, dig the garden, mow the lawn, do the family shopping. But when he told me to sweep the chimney I left."'

However, there was one veterinary graduate in the cold month of December 1939 who did not have to worry about getting a job in the profession. Mr J. A. Wight MRCVS had already been offered a post: he was going back to the town of his birth as assistant to none other than Jock McDowall, at the kingly wage of £3-3s a week. As to his board, he could stay with Auntie Jinny around the corner at Beechwood Terrace. He had to leave Don behind, though.

Arriving at McDowall's familiar surgery for his first day's work, Alf was greeted with a hearty welcome by McDowall. 'Welcome to Sunderland, Fred! [For some reason McDowall always called Alf 'Fred'.] These small animals are the things that pay.'

The rise and rise of the pet was one of the changes that would turn the world of James Herriot upside down. Although today around 80 per cent of veterinary time is spent with small animals, with less than 5 per cent of veterinary surgeons involved full time with farm animal work, in the Thirties the proportions were almost exactly reversed.

By some cruel humour of the Fates – or of their new employers – newly qualified vets always start in at the very deepest end. Thus Alf's career began with an emergency: almost as soon as McDowall had uttered the words 'Small animals pay!' he was taken ill with virulent flu, leaving Alf to run the practice solo. As Alf had not yet passed his driving test, a doddery friend of McDowall's had to be hired as chauffeur for farm visits. Running McDowall's show, however, turned out to be the very least of Alf's problems. The reason McDowall could afford to pay Alf was because of his post as 'veterinary surgeon in attendance' at South Shield's dog racing tracks. He had warned Alf that the finances of the stadium were parlous, and should it close Alf would have to go.

Less than a fortnight after Alf arrived in Sunderland, McDowall learned that the stadium faced closure. Lacking the money to pay Alf, he had to advise his new assistant to seek work elsewhere. An unusually subdued Alf Wight wrote to his parents on 14 January 1940:

My dear Mother and Dad,

I'm afraid I have some bad news and I may as well get it over with. I didn't get the job at Guisborough. McDonald, the vet there, received an application from a man from Skye and as he is from Skye himself that was that. Don't be too despondent about this; it's a big disappointment but remember that fellows like me are being turned down all over the country. Mac's ill and won't be up for a few days so I'll be OK for another week's pay, but after that, what?

If it's all the same to you folks I think it would be better if I stayed on here even though I get no more pay. You see, I get free driving practice, I'm in touch with veterinary affairs and, most important of all, I would get no chance to get rusty and stale as I would at home with nowt to do. Here, I'm learning every day and there is just a chance that Mac might slip me something now and again towards my board. Don't be too upset about the job, something may turn up.

As to recreation, I have had none and haven't seen any of my friends and relatives. I get home just in time for a game of cards with George and then early to bed. Mac hasn't given me my pay yet but he slipped me a quid on account at the beginning of the week so I was able to get Auntie Jinny a bottle of lavender water for her birthday.

Love Alf

P.S. Feeling fine!

Ten days later, though, Alf was back in employment with Mac. The National Greyhound Racing Board had now decided to revitalize the Sunderland stadium, with Mac taken on as veterinary adviser. Alf's wages went up to £4-4s per week. For once he was able to treat his parents, sending home 30s from his pay, adding 'Buy yourself 10 Woodbines, Pop old boy!'

To put the cherry on the icing of Alf's cake, he then passed his driving test, although his delight was somewhat lessened when he saw the car McDowall had secured for him to drive around the practice; it was a standard model for young vets in the Thirties, a tiny tinny Ford with reluctant brakes and an engine which made 'a colossal din' and startled birds and horses alike. 'The vibration is terrific over 35 mph,' he told his parents, 'and my liver will be in splendid condition after a month.'

But Alf gradually decided that Sunderland was not the place for a long-term veterinary career. McDowall continued to be unpleasantly explosive, a question mark still hung over the greyhound stadium despite all the fine words, and the wind whipping off the grey North Sea made the town infinitely dreary in winter. He began perusing the scant advertisements in the *Veterinary Record*.

One day, leafing through, he saw a post advertised in Thirsk. 'Mainly agricultural work in a Yorkshire market town' was the job description. Perhaps there would be green and pleasant hills…The principal of the practice at 23 Kirkgate was a graduate of the Royal ('Dick') College, Donald Sinclair MRCVS. Eventually, after finding Thirsk on the map, about 50 miles south of Sunderland, Alf thought the job would do, and set pen to paper.

Dear Mr Farnon…

BIBLIOGRAPHY

PRIMARY SOURCES

J. A. Wight, *The Art and the Science*, unpublished novel

J. A. Wight Diary 1933

J. A. Wight Diary 1934 (transcribed by Margaret Tipton)

J. A. Wight Casebook 'Practice Seen with TB Fleming MRCVS during 1937'

J. A. Wight Casebook 'Cases Seen with Mr JJ McDowall MRCVS' 1938

Interview with K. Mitchell 2011

Interview with Jim Wight 2011

Interview with Rosie Page 2011

Interview with Peter Jinman, OBE MRCVS 2011

Interview with Nigel Carter

Nigel Carter 'Recipe Book'

DCC 144/5/1/1 Inventory and Valuation: The Glasgow Veterinary College (Incorporated), December 1937, Glasgow University

DCC 144/3/2/2 Register of Students No. 2, Glasgow University

DCC 144/3/5/2 Register of Students' Class Marks, Glasgow University

SECONDARY SOURCES

Anonymous, *Hillhead High School 1885–1961*, 1962

Anonymous, *Veterinary Counter Practice*, 1930

Anonymous, 'Mary Brancker', Obituaries, *Daily Telegraph*, 30 July 2010

Anonymous, *Glasgow Veterinary School 1862–1962*, 1962

Edward Boden, 'Dame Olga Uvarov', *Independent*, 7 July 2001

– 'Practice and Politics: the British Veterinary Association 1881–1919' www.bva.co.uk/public/documents/BVA_history_1881-1919.pdf

John Carroll and Garry Stuart, *Tractors*, 2002

Helen Clark and Elizabeth Carnegie, *She Was Aye Workin'*, 2003

David Daiches, *Glasgow*, 1982

Jean Faley, *Up Oor Close*, 1990

Thomas Firbank, *I Bought a Mountain*, 1959

Connie M. Ford, *Aleen Cust*, 1990

Ernest A. Gray, 'John Hunter and Veterinary Medicine', *Medical History*, January 1957

James Herriot, *If Only They Could Talk*, 1970

– *It Shouldn't Happen to a Vet*, 1972

– *Let Sleeping Vets Lie*, 1973

– *Vet in Harness*, 1974

– *Vets Might Fly*, 1976

– *Vet in a Spin*, 1977

– *The Lord God Made Them All*, 1981

– *Every Living Thing*, 1992

– *James Herriot's Yorkshire*, 1979

– *James Herriot's Dog Stories*, 1986

Miles Horsey, *Tenements & Towers*, 1990

Pamela Hunter, *Veterinary Medicine: A Guide to the Historical Sources*, 2004

Robert Jeffrey, *Gangs of Glasgow*, 2002

Rudolph Kenna and Ian Sutherland, *They Belonged to Glasgow*, 2001

Margaret Leigh, *Highland Homespun*, 1936

Graham Lord, *James Herriot: The Life of a Country Vet*, 1997

James McCunn, *Hobday's Surgical Diseases of The Dog and Cat*, 1947

Alan McKinlay, *Making Ships, Making Men: Working for John Brown's – Between the Wars*, 1991

Meccano Magazine, December 1931

William C. Miller, *Black's Veterinary Dictionary*, 1928

H. O. Monnig, *Veterinary Helminthology and Entomology*, 1938

H. V. Morton, *In Search of Scotland*, 1929

J. P. Muller, *My System*, 1931

C. A. Oakley, *The Second City*, 1967

Iain Pattison, *John Mcfadyean*, 1981

Hugh B. Peebles, *Warship Building on the Clyde*, 1987

J. M. Reid, *Glasgow*, 1956

Michael J. Rossi, *James Herriot: A Critical Companion*, 1997

J. A. Scott Watson, *The Farming Year*, 1938

Eddie Straiton, *Animals Are My Life*, 1979

Fred M. Walker, *Song of the Clyde*, 1984

Ralph Whitlock, *A Short History of Farming in Britain*, 1966

William T. W. Wells, *A Handy Book of Reference for Farmers in Scotland*, 1920

Jim Wight, *The Real James Herriot*, 1999

ACKNOWLEDGEMENTS

James Herriot's children, Rosie Page and Jim Wight; the staff at The World of James Herriot, Thirsk; Kate Croft at Shed Media; Albert DePetrillo and Laura Higginson at BBC Books; Georgia Glover at David Higham; Julian Alexander, Ben Clark, Petra Lewis at Lucas Alexander Whitley; Peter Jinman OBE, MRCVS, President of the Royal College of Veterinary Surgeons; Ken Mitchell; Nigel Carter; the staff of the Mitchell Library, Glasgow; the staff of the Archives, Glasgow University.

I am also grateful to J. A. Allen for permission to reprint extracts from Eddie Straiton's *Animals Are My Life*, and to Sovereign Books for permission to reprint extracts from Hugh Lasgarn's *Vet in Green Pastures*.

But my greatest thanks go to my wife, Penny Lewis-Stempel, without whom I would never have started, let alone finished.

INDEX

(AW indicates Alf Wight.)